...eople

CHOICES

GUIDES FOR TODAY'S WOMAN

Other People

Mary Jo Meadow

The Westminster Press
Philadelphia

Copyright © 1984 Mary Jo Meadow

Book Design by Alice Derr

First edition

Published by The Westminster Press ®
Philadelphia, Pennsylvania

PRINTED IN THE UNITED STATES OF AMERICA
9 8 7 6 5 4 3 2 1

Library of Congress Cataloging in Publication Data

Meadow, Mary Jo, date
   Other people.

   (Choices)
   1. Interpersonal relations. 2. Interpersonal communication. 3. Social psychology. I. Title. II. Series.
HM132.M375 1984   302.3′4   84-2315
ISBN 0-664-24544-7 (pbk.)

*This book is lovingly dedicated
to the memory of Grandma,
Mabel Elise Ryan Strupper (1884–1972)*

CONTENTS

PUBLISHER'S ACKNOWLEDGMENT

The publisher gratefully acknowledges the advice of several distinguished scholars in planning this series. Virginia Mollenkott, Arlene Swidler, Phyllis Trible, and Ann Ulanov helped shape the goals of the series, identify vital topics, and locate knowledgeable authors. Views expressed in the books, of course, are those of the individual writers and not of the advisers.

PREFACE

We all want to get along with other people. Although we don't choose to be close to all people, we want to avoid unnecessary conflict when dealing with them. Most people remember painful experiences with others as some of life's worst events.

This book is mainly about our relationships with people with whom we don't establish intimate ties but must be involved. Some such people may later become friends, but most remain a small part of our busy lives. Some of these relationships go smoothly, but others are filled with problems because of individual differences in style, likes, dislikes, values, and goals. Although this book focuses chiefly on getting along with problem people, studying it will help all your relationships.

You will learn how all people work, including yourself, and also why we differ in so many ways. Many relationship problems occur because one person jars another's hopes and expectations about how she should be or behave. The different ways in which people are reared, and the temperamental differences among us, create most of these difficulties. Understanding this human variety can lead to overall relationship improvement.

This book will also teach you how to be understood

when you communicate with others and how to help them express themselves clearly. It will teach you things about yourself and others that help lay the basis for a solid and healthy love of self and others. It will help you recognize hidden self-centeredness and manipulation before they destroy relationships. My hope is that it will lead you to helpful, supportive, and cooperative relationships, and that you will feel greater ease and satisfaction in dealing with other people.

I thank my publisher, Westminster Press, for help in producing this book. I also thank my friends, students, clients, and colleagues whose stories—with names changed—illuminate the text. Finally, a special note of thanks goes to Grandma, to whom this book is dedicated. A strong, courageous, and competent woman, she dearly loved me and filled me with an eager desire to learn, understand, and share the fruits of my scholarship with others.

M.J.M.

CHAPTER 1

Understanding and Communicating with People

More Flies are taken with a Drop of Honey
   than a Tun of Vinegar.
      —Thomas Fuller, *Gnomologia*

Some general principles about why we act as we do and how we communicate will start this exploration of dealing with other people. These principles give us help in understanding and managing all relationships, particularly difficult ones.

WHAT MAKES PEOPLE TICK

SOME PSYCHOLOGICAL PRINCIPLES

Even if we believe there is more to people than psychology can explain, studying psychological functioning helps us understand much of our behavior. We now look at some important ideas about motivation.

The Pleasure Principle. The outcomes of what people do strongly affect what they are most likely to do again. We work according to "the pleasure principle." We do things that bring us satisfying results, and we do not do things that don't. If Sally feels good about herself when she is with Linda, she will tend to choose being with Linda. If Martha pretty much ignores Carolyn, Carolyn is not likely to seek out her company. You can probably easily think of some people you seek out and others you don't.

Some religious people might protest that the only people who work that way are those whose "god is their belly" (Phil. 3:19), or who are otherwise not tuned into spiritual values. Those whose treasure is with the things of God (Matt. 6:21) will act on religious values rather than pleasure. They may even choose painful or uncomfortable things because they see them as a duty, or as the more appropriate choice for a religious person. They may choose to be with some unrewarding people because they feel they should.

If this sounds like what you would say, stop and think for a minute. When religious values become a major motivation in your life, you have simply changed what gives you satisfaction. You still do what satisfies you, but that is different from what satisfies some other people. You might even "enjoy" self-sacrifice or suffering when doing it to serve God or another person, but this still follows the pleasure principle. Hindus say that people at different levels of spiritual development act, in turn, for pleasure, power, duty, and making themselves an offering to God. As people mature spiritually, what most satisfies them changes, but they still act for satisfaction.

Basic Human Needs. Even those who commit their lives to religious values do not always choose them over other goods. We all have ordinary human needs that demand satisfaction when not filled. A strong unmet need can pretty easily take over your entire being. Perhaps you remember being so sleepy that sleeping was the only thing appealing to you. Most of us can recall times when we felt so insecure or isolated that these feelings dominated our thoughts and made it almost impossible to attend to anything else.

Psychologist Abraham Maslow listed our basic needs. These are given in Box 1.1, with some situations that can activate each need.

BOX 1.1
MASLOW'S BASIC NEEDS

Basic Need	Some Situations Triggering the Need
Physiological	hunger and thirst cold, heat, pain sleepiness, fatigue
Safety	being threatened by a real or imaginary danger being in an unfamiliar place being uncertain of your understanding of a situation
Belongingness	feeling "left out" of things or ignored feeling out of place and not fitting in being where you don't know anyone else
Love	lacking friends or close affectional ties with others feeling uncared for or unloved not being able to show caring or love for others
Esteem	being treated with lack of respect having your ideas or feelings laughed at being scolded, lectured, or ordered about
Self-Esteem	knowing you have violated your values feeling inadequate in dealing with a situation feeling less important, valuable, or good than others
Self-Actualization	being kept from developing a talent or ability lacking suitable and satisfying lifework failing to understand yourself and how you work
Self-Transcendence	failing to develop a unifying philosophy of life failing to choose and live by higher values living as if you are the center of the universe (or God)

These needs are in a hierarchy; that means that a badly unsatisfied lower need dominates over a higher one. After a need has been consistently satisfied for a while, we can better put up with it when it is not. Our history has left us expecting that the need will eventually be met. For example, you now wait more easily for a meal when you are hungry than you did when you were five years old. However, serious need eventually takes over. Even in adult maturity, if hungry enough, most of us bend all our energies toward getting food before doing anything else.

Maslow's view of human nature was very positive. He believed that if people are encouraged, and lower level needs are met, they will naturally progress to higher needs. Whether this is true or not, our experiences show us how lower level needs can preoccupy us and block out higher motives. Sometimes higher motives can temporarily override lower needs and make us tolerate lack of satisfaction longer. If I get very involved in my writing—a self-actualization need (see Box 1.1)—and it is going well, I might get very hungry before I am willing to stop to eat. Some people put up with a lot of fear (safety needs not satisfied) to "save face" (an esteem need).

Many religious people try to make religious values important enough to override all other motives. Someone who always makes religious values win out over lower level needs is a saint. However, only very rarely do we find someone like Maximilian Kolbe who starved to death in a Nazi concentration camp to buy another prisoner's freedom.

Maslow said we must actively seek need gratification. We cannot sit and wait for someone else to do it for us. Thus, if love needs are unmet, a person should try to show love to others; giving love is every bit as important as receiving it to satisfy this need. Indeed, giving love often makes one so lovable that she finds herself receiving a lot of it! Not moving to higher level needs affects a person's mental health. We can become neurotic from failing to deal with such higher needs as self-esteem, self-actualization, and self-transcendence. According to Maslow, one of the strongest causes of neurosis in our culture is that bright women so often wind up doing "stupid" work.

Sensitivity to other people's unmet needs helps us work effectively with them. Much of the time, most people are preoccupied with unmet lower needs. That is, most people cannot be moved by higher order motives because lower level priorities have not been satisfied. Any wife who feeds her husband dinner before asking for something she wants understands this. A hungry person is less likely to be moved by love than one who has been fed!

Emotional Associations. If you figure out what a person's most pressing unmet need is, and satisfy that need, you can become very satisfying to that person. Revolutionaries, reformers, and missionaries who offer food and medicine before preaching their ideology know this. Another principle of psychology explains how this works.

Anything associated with something very pleasant or unpleasant tends to make us feel as that pleasant or unpleasant thing did. One of my high school classmates was a very slovenly girl named Loretta. Although many people consider Loretta an attractive name, I have never liked it because it draws up images of this very messy Loretta. The song "When I Fall in Love" draws loneliness—linked with adolescent longings for the boyfriend I did not have. The sight and sound of trains bring me both a nostalgic elation and a missing of Grandma; she and I spent many happy hours together on trains when I was a child.

Think about the effect that different colors, smells, first names, aspects of nature, places, types of people, foods, buildings, and so on have on you. Did an Oriental woman comfort you when you were lost in a department store as a small child? I'll bet you have strong positive feelings toward Oriental women. Did you experience deep spiritual peace at a particular chapel or sanctuary? You must sometimes yearn to be back there. Were you frightened by a group of adolescent boys on a trip into the city? You probably fear and resent adolescent boys. Do you have a favorite color? With what is it associated? Are certain foods especially appealing or distasteful? Where did you have them before?

Recall that people work by the pleasure principle, and tend to repeat experiences that bring them positive outcomes. These positive experiences are called reinforcers. Some things, such as food, sex, rest when tired, being stroked, seem to be built in biologically as reinforcers. Many other things become reinforcers because they are associated with other positive experiences; money and praise are good examples. Similarly, we learn to want to avoid certain other things. By getting yourself associated with other people's positive experiences, such as need satisfaction, you become a reinforcer—something positive and desirable to people with whom you must deal.

USING THESE IDEAS

We now have three important psychological principles for understanding both yourself and other people. First is the pleasure principle—that we do what satisfies us. Second is that the needs most important to us move us, and we seek their fulfillment. These range from biological needs to the need to actualize chosen values in our lives. Satisfying needs is pleasurable. Third, things associated with either very positive or negative experiences tend to take on the feeling tone of those experiences. Things associated with positive experiences appeal to us, while those associated with negative events drive us away.

How does this apply to dealing with people who may be difficult? These three principles together give us very powerful tools for improving these relationships. First, we can try to understand what in ourselves makes us find them difficult. We will talk more about this later. Sometimes it is actually how others behave toward us, but sometimes we "hang" things on them that have nothing to do with them personally. I would be doing that if I instantly dislike someone named Loretta. Second, we can make ourselves appealing to them. If we meet their unmet needs, they will feel good and we will be associated with that pleasure. (Although these principles are solid ones, sometimes things do not work quite so simply. We will talk in later chapters about some complications.)

Can these ideas be used to manipulate others? You bet they can! It is very scary to realize how much control we can have over other people by applying these principles. Many con artists and manipulators know them. Some "people pleasers"—those who need always to be approved of by others—have discovered these ideas. However, these methods can also be used by people who are genuinely interested in improving relationships to benefit both themselves and others. When you figure out what other people's needs are and meet them, you do them a service. We could even say that you are "loving" them, although you still might not like all of them! You release them from being "hung up" on a lower need so that they can attend to higher motives. It makes sense that they will be grateful to you and find you a satisfying person.

HOW TO COMMUNICATE

How often people complain about someone to a counselor: "She just doesn't care about me or she'd understand how I feel!" Or, "She goes out of her way to hurt me when we try to talk." Or, "I simply can't get through to her no matter how hard I try." You have probably heard yourself or someone else say such things. Communication is a difficult art. Effective communication does not come naturally to many people, yet our education seldom includes learning these skills.

What Can Be Communicated

We see many things about others that they also know about themselves. We may know some other things about a person that she does not know about herself. Luann's slip may be showing, or Dee may have food on the side of her mouth. Perhaps Pam usually tacks "you know" onto what she says, or Beth always licks her lips before she speaks. However, we cannot know another's interior mental and emotional state unless she tells us. So, although others notice much about us of which we may be unaware, so also much cannot be known by them unless we tell them. Finally, some things about us are seen neither by us nor by other people. A design called a Johari window diagrams these different aspects of an individual person. Box 1.2 has one for you.

You cannot know the things in the "Blind" box unless others tell you. "Open" things are not hidden from anyone. You are aware of them, and others can also see them. They may need to be discussed if they bother someone, but everyone can count on their being known. "Unconscious" things might influence your actions, but cannot be discussed since neither you nor others are aware of them. Some unconscious things move without

BOX 1.2
YOUR JOHARI WINDOW

	You See	You Don't See
Others See	**Open** what you say to others your expressed ideas chosen behavior shared, expressed feelings choice of clothes hairstyle	**Blind** many of your mannerisms habitual gestures patterns in your behavior facial expressions nervous habits some others' reactions to you
Others Don't See	**Secret** your private fantasies unexpressed wishes "hidden sins" unshared fears and doubts unshared resentments unshared goals and dreams	**Unconscious** forgotten memories unaware motives emotional tendencies perceptual habits "repressed" hurts "instinctive" movements

effort into another of the boxes. Your actions can give others clues to these things about you, or else your self-awareness may increase and you see hidden things about yourself that you hadn't recognized before. When too many important determiners of your conduct are not known to you, a therapist can sometimes help.

What is "Secret" is private to you unless you share it. We don't share all that is important about ourselves with everyone else. However, remember that others don't have this information unless you do share it. If it involves someone else—a plan, motive, or decision that will affect her—sharing it helps the relationship, and not sharing it can hurt. If you just refuse to take Mia shopping whenever she asks you, she will eventually get the point, but at risk to the relationship. Saying, "I have decided that I can't take you shopping anymore because it takes too much time," is better. Then you can deal openly with feelings about it. Of course, you do not share private things with people who will use them against you. You do not say, "I am feeling terrible because I failed my Civil Service exam," to someone who will blab it all over town.

How to Get Through Clearly

Leveling and Confronting. Sharing our inner private lives is called leveling. I level with you when I let you know what is going on inside me regarding some issue. Leveling requires appropriate honesty and frankness.

When I confront you, I tell you things I have noticed that I think you do not see or are not sufficiently considering. I might confront you about something of which you are aware, but did not realize the implications of. For example, "Do you realize that you've been at least fifteen minutes late the last dozen times we've met?" Poorly handled confronting sometimes leads to an argument, and sometimes confronting is inappropriate. Not all confronting is negative in tone. I once asked a colleague, "Do you realize how soft and gentle your voice becomes when you talk to one of your students?"

Like most good things, confronting and leveling can be misused. Sharing feelings or plans to manipulate another person is an obvious misuse of leveling. I am being seriously dishonest with myself if I call it necessary confronting when I say things meant to hurt another person. Before confronting or leveling, a good practice is to ask yourself what your motives are, what you want to accomplish. This helps you distinguish misuse from such appropriate motives as solving a relationship problem, increasing closeness with another, telling another your plans that affect her, helping another realize important things about herself, or increasing mutual understanding.

One particularly useful practice, especially when confronting with criticism, is to sugarcoat it. This is not dishonest. Most criticisms have related positive features. If you can think of nothing positive about the confrontation issue, think of some other relevant positive communication with which to begin. A university administrator said to me: "Mary Jo, your contagious enthusiasm and energetic hard work really help to move projects along when you get involved in them. But did you realize that sometimes other people feel pushed too fast by you, and that you have taken charge of things before they even know what is going on?" His tactful presentation of this perception made it easier for me to listen to him, and to become sensitive to situations where his criticism was valid.

You can level in ways that don't hurt another's feelings, even when the message is negative. Being very clear and definite is important. A garbled message or mere hinting may leave the other person confused about what your feelings or intentions really are. Harriet said to Vivian: "My life is so busy right now that I don't have enough time to see people who are already very dear to me. So I'm not open to our trying a friendship, but I do appreciate your asking." This is honest, clearly understood, and definite, and does not discount the other person. Also, although Vivian didn't tempt Harriet from this position, Harriet can allow someone else to do so, if she wishes.

Mind-Reading and Checking Out. Some people expect others to know what is going on inside of them without being told; they think others should be able to read their minds! Although this sounds silly when said so bluntly, most of us can remember at least thinking—if we didn't actually say—something like this: "I shouldn't have to tell her how I am feeling because she would know if she really cared about me."

Barbara had just come from the doctor and was so happy to learn she was pregnant that she was sure her joy must be written all over her face. When she and Susan met for lunch, Susan started excitedly talking about her new project, which meant an automatic promotion. The more she talked, the more despondent Barbara became. She had been expecting Susan to "magically" know that she was eager to share news. Susan, who did not make such assumptions, was caught up in her own big news. By the time she asked Barbara—who had become sullen and silent—how things were going for her, Barbara was so "hurt" that she didn't even want to tell Susan. Barbara failed to realize that our own lives are the only ones always immediately present to us; however interested and concerned another may be about us, she cannot accurately read our every mood and expression.

Because we do sometimes "mind read" others, without checking out whether we are correct, we make serious mistakes. Jean stomped past Ruth without even nodding or smiling. Then she sat down with her arms folded across her chest and said nothing during the entire meeting. Like many people would, Ruth asked herself why Jean should be angry with her. When she couldn't figure it out, she decided that Jean must be terribly unreasonable for being angry over something so small that she, Ruth, couldn't even remember it. (Notice that Ruth had definitely concluded that Jean was angry with her.) Ruth herself got so angry that she planned to snub Jean, disrupting their friendship. Then she remembered checking out. After the meeting, she asked: "Jean, you haven't even noticed me since you got here. Is something wrong that I don't know about?" Had Jean been angry with Ruth, she had an opportunity to explain.

However, she looked very startled and said: "Oh, I'm sorry, Ruth. I honestly didn't even see you. I'm so mad at the plumber who didn't show up that I can't seem to think of anything else." Obviously, checking out is important when we are tempted to draw conclusions about what another person is thinking or feeling!

It is important to check out when you are not sure that someone really understood what you said, or that you understood what she said. Ione did this when she said: "Sandy, I want to be sure you understood me. What did you hear me saying?" Sandy answered, "Well, if you don't want to go with me, that's okay." (Can you tell that this indirect, evasive answer may be masking hurt feelings?) Ione explained: "I didn't say I don't want to go with you. I said that I'm too busy Friday to add anything to my schedule. Perhaps I can go with you the next time."

If Ione really did not want to go, she might say: "Sandy, that just doesn't interest me. It doesn't mean that I don't want to spend time with you, though, and I'm afraid that's what you think. Is it?" If Sandy answered, "Well, it sounded like that to me"; Ione could say, "Let's plan something together we'll both enjoy." Had Ione not checked out, Sandy would have left feeling rejected.

I-Statements and You-Statements. Compare these two requests. (1) "Slow down, please, before you kill all of us." (2) "Driving this fast really scares me. Please slow down." The second request is much more likely to get good results. The first one makes you-statements. It says something about the person being addressed—that she is foolish, careless, putting you in danger. The second request says something about the speaker; it makes an I-statement. It levels about the speaker's emotional reactions.

Generally, I-statements work better than you-statements when dealing with another person, even when saying something positive. "I really like that dress on you" is a stronger compliment than "Your dress is very pretty." "I felt so good when your card came" is better than "You are such a thoughtful person." To call another nice names, or say that she has good qualities, may leave her feeling hollow because she knows it is not *all* true; at times she is not thoughtful. But your feelings cannot be disputed. She cannot diminish your pleasure; she must either accept it, or call you a liar. She doesn't have to think, "Well, maybe I was thoughtful this time, but I know I am not always." She can rejoice that she has made her friend happy with the card.

Saying "Don't you think it would be better to ... " forces the other person to agree that your thoughts are hers, or else to challenge you. If you say, "It seems to me it would be better to ... What do you think?", you let the other person know your opinion, and leave her free to express her own.

"Would you like to go to a movie?" is a poor way to state your own preference. The other person may feel manipulated into saying she is interested for fear you will feel rebuffed if she doesn't. "I want to go to a movie tonight. Will you go with me?" lets the other person either gracefully decline or accept without having to call it her own preference.

COMMUNICATING DIFFICULT FEELINGS

Some of the most difficult communication problems occur when people are strongly aroused emotionally, or when they see things very differently. Good communication skills can ease these situations.

Anger. Sometimes, when anger is intense, the wisest course is to call a moratorium on discussion until both parties cool down. If one stays more calm and cool than the other, this can fuel the other's anger. Although you need not yell or be abusive, overcontrolling your reactions may leave the other person feeling "shown up" or inadequate: "There you stand, cool as a cucumber, all together, and you make me look like a raving idiot!" Although another may not say this, she could be feeling it.

If you are angry, a clear admission of it and an honest statement of why are most helpful. In giving your reasons, stick to the current issues involved; don't bring up that Abby spilled a glass of wine on your new dress two years ago. Talk about the particular problem, and not the other's character. This also involves making I-statements instead of you-statements. You might say: "I am really angry. I feel treated very unfairly when I'm kept waiting in the rain for twenty minutes. If the delay was unavoidable, I would have appreciated a phone call." (Note such subtleties as "I would have appreciated a phone call" instead of "You at least could have called.") Obviously, this is better than: "You are so inconsiderate. You've kept me waiting in the rain for twenty minutes. Don't you know how to use a phone? Well, what could I expect! You never even offered to have my dress cleaned when you spilled your drink all over it." Although this last speech sounds overdone, very often people make at least some of its mistakes.

Guilt. Guilt is an uncomfortable emotion, and sometimes people hide behind anger—projecting blame on another—to avoid it. If you forgot to run a promised errand for a friend, you may get angry that she asked you to do it. When another is angry with you, guilt may be underneath her rage.

When a guilty person apologizes, we often reassure her in unhelpful ways. When Marilyn declined to have dinner with her, Toni said that she desperately needed to talk to her. So, to help her friend, Marilyn agreed to meet her. After some time, when Toni did not bring up any "heavy" issues, Marilyn asked what was bothering her. Toni guiltily admitted that she had just been very lonely, and didn't have any specific issues. Then she apologized and asked Marilyn not to be angry. Marilyn, who wants to make others feel good, said: "Oh, don't feel so bad. That's okay. I understand."

Such a reply is less helpful than one that makes the relationship more honest. Marilyn might have said: "I'd really prefer your being honest when you want to see me. I have an important report due tomorrow and would rather have just talked on the phone if you were lonely. My need to get the report done is probably at least as important as yours for company." Then, if she wished, Marilyn could let Toni know that the relationship had not been ruptured. You can accept an apology without minimizing the impact and consequences of the other's bad behavior. Too much understanding often makes a guilty person feel even worse, and leaves issues unresolved.

Fear. Many fears interfere with clear communication between people: fears of rejection, misunderstanding, vulnerability, betrayal, abandonment, loss of esteem or love, and many others. Fear also may come out as anger. Often people fluctuate between the two. Perhaps your teenage child is seriously overdue on curfew. You probably go back and forth between fear that something bad has happened, and anger at being treated inconsiderately. Often, when the child comes home and the fear is relieved, all the anger pours out. Admitting the fear also would probably lead to more considerate behavior from the teenager than anger alone does. Acknowledging fear is usually harder than being angry because it leaves us much more vulnerable. However, it usually gets better results.

Cindy seemed somewhat annoyed, so Holly decided to check it out. Cindy replied, "Well, you told me you were going to call me last week." Holly thought she detected a hint of fear that the friendship was losing its importance to her. She replied: "I did plan to. I am really sorry. My son's emergency surgery kept me so preoccupied that I simply forgot almost everything else." This response quieted Cindy's fear, and she was immediately "normal" Cindy again. Had Holly responded tartly to Cindy's anger—"Well, I told you I was busy last week with my son's surgery. Surely, you can't expect ... " (a reply that also makes you-statements)—the situation would not have been as easily resolved. Holly may still need to deal with Cindy's insecurity in the friendship, though.

SUMMARY

These examples show how a few simple changes in wording can greatly improve communication and relationships with others. The key words to remember are checking out, leveling, confronting, and I-statements. Also important in improving relationships is honesty about how your own needs and past experiences color your response to others. Such self-understanding also increases understanding of others. The next chapter explores this factor.

CHAPTER 2

How Life Experiences Make People Different

'Tis education forms the common mind:
Just as the twig is bent, the tree's inclined.
—Alexander Pope, *Moral Essays* I

Why haven't all the things discussed in Chapter 1 made much difference in how people get along? Why do such ideas so often fail to work? One reason is that people have many different life experiences, especially in our early years when we are most shaped by what happens to us. Although some experiences help us learn to manage life, others teach us bad ways to deal with the issues we face.

Our direct education comes from school, our parents' spoken words, and our churches. This is only a small part of all we learn, though. We also learn important things from watching others live their lives and from our feelings about events in our lives. This learning, commonly not in full awareness, often causes trouble in getting along with other people.

THINGS WE LEARN BY WATCHING OTHERS

Transactional analysis says that before we are five years old we collect thousands of hours of "tapes" in our minds giving us a basic approach to life. This "taught way of life" affects how we see, understand, and value things. In later life, we then make such decisions without knowing we are doing so. We think we are seeing what is really "out there," but we are only looking at the pictures we have painted on it, all the changes we make in it to have it match our understandings.

HOW WE LEARN BY WATCHING

June seemed unable to make or keep good friendships with women. She felt that the problem was that you just can't trust other women beyond a certain point. Nobody directly taught this to June. But June grew up seeing her mother's inability to trust women, and heard her mother repeat stories about how women's rivalries lead them to "do in" a friend rather than lose out on anything. June heard no stories about good relationships between women. She clearly got the message not to trust women. Is it any wonder that she cannot have a good friendship with a woman?

The Idea of Modeling. "Modeling" describes how we are affected by what we see others do. A child's most powerful early models are her parents. We saw that June learned simply by watching and listening to her mother deal with women. June never questioned her mother's perceptions. This learning got so deeply ingrained that she took it for granted as true. Much of what is modeled for us early in life works that way.

Acting like a "Parent." There are ways to tell when other people are trying to impose their taught way of life on you—and when you are trying to load yours on them. When doing this, we tend to use words like "should," "must," "ought," "always," and "never." When you say, "Zoe really should . . . ," you are trying to impose your understandings on her. When people shake their finger at another, or wrinkle their brow while talking, they are often trying to "parent" the other person. Being aware of these signals helps us avoid some relationship problems this causes. By listening to your own shoulds, you start understanding which ideas you might want to impose on others. By listening to theirs, you get an idea of their assumptions about life and people.

How What We Learn This Way Affects Us

Our taught way of life makes us see situations in our own unique way. It also leaves us with many expectations about how other people should act.

The Right Way and the Wrong Way. Much of our taught way of life says how to do ordinary tasks. A story is told about newlyweds cooking a ham. The bride insisted on cutting the ham in half before cooking it, and the groom couldn't understand why. When the bride explained that her mother *always* cooked ham that way, they agreed to ask the mother why when they next saw her. The mother said that her mother had *always* cooked ham that way. When the newlyweds, still arguing about how to cook ham, finally asked the grandmother, she answered, "Oh, I did that because I never had a pan large enough to hold a whole ham!" This story shows well how we take for granted, as the "right way" to do something, how we saw it done by important other people.

Always and Never. Some expectations are not seen as having any alternatives at all. On Paula's first day with us as a mother's helper, she asked if I wanted her to start the potatoes for dinner. When I told her that we weren't having potatoes that night, she didn't seem to grasp what I was saying. After a few minutes of confusion, she finally blurted out, "But you *always* have potatoes for dinner!" For Paula, no other options existed for a dinner meal. Can you think of some things for which you see no alternatives?

Rituals. When Bobbi didn't send Rhoda a birthday card, she was crushed. Bobbi could see that Rhoda was hurt, but she didn't understand what was wrong. When Rhoda finally told her what hurt her, Bobbi was flabbergasted. Rhoda's mother always sent birthday cards to her friends, while Bobbi's mother had never done such a thing. Both had learned ways to celebrate a friend's birthday—and they were different ways.

We learn many rituals—ways to celebrate important days and events—from how our families did it. We also learn rituals for conducting friendships, organizing meetings, working together in groups, and deciding lines of responsibility. When people try to work together—or simply get along in any relationship—these different rituals can make trouble. Others may be seen as insensitive, rude, uncaring, tactless, or even evil when their expectations about these rituals differ from our own.

The "Oughts" of Life. The oughts are very important in a "learned way of life." They range from deeply held moral convictions to simpler ideas about how we want to be treated. Leigh planned to meet a friend at a convention. When she went to the message board where they were to meet, she found a very angry message from her friend: "I know you have been at this meeting at least a full day because someone saw you and told me. I would have thought that you at least could have left me a note welcoming me since you knew I would be coming later." Leigh's friend was unusually sensitive to an imagined rebuff, but was genuinely hurt because of how she thought Leigh should behave.

Differences about oughts get even more touchy when they involve moral convictions. Lynn and Jan are neighbors who share many interests and enjoy each other's company. They quickly learned to avoid discussing nuclear weapons to keep their friendship. Jan's family taught her that national defense must be top priority, regardless of costs. Lynn grew up believing that any warfare was the height of moral irresponsibility.

PREJUDICE

Prejudice is prejudgment. Transactional analysis says that it occurs when our taught way of life keeps us from clearly seeing things. We have set expectations—often negative ones—of other people because of their gender, race, ethnicity, religion, or other group membership. Such expectations are often not openly taught us, but are picked up by observing the prejudices of important people in our early lives.

When I first began teaching, one woman asked to talk to me after class halfway through the quarter. She looked ill at ease, and said she did not know how to tell me what she had to say. I encouraged her and finally she said: "I'm so embarrassed! The first night of class when you walked in, I was furious. I said, 'Here I finally decide to take another class, and I have to get a woman teacher.' I felt really cheated. Now I have to tell you that this is about the best class I've ever had. I'm so ashamed I was automatically expecting it to be bad because a woman was teaching it."

This woman had learned a prejudice—that women do not do university teaching as well as men—but she was not so prejudiced that she couldn't change her mind. Unfortunately, some people are so prejudiced that they cannot be changed. Since prejudices seriously distort our perceptions of reality, they greatly handicap us in dealing with people. Seeing our own prejudices is hard because we are so convinced that they are real. Any time you expect certain good or bad experiences with a person you do not yet know, you are probably having prejudiced expectations of a group into which they fit.

Sometimes prejudices make a person who is unsure of

herself feel better. They give her someone to look down on. This makes recognizing and getting rid of prejudices even harder. The most prejudiced people are insecure and rigid. They deal with their doubts and fears by looking down on others, blaming others for what goes wrong, and having dogmatic opinions. Knowing that such a woman is not comfortable with herself makes it easier to control anger at her. She will not be helped by harsh and demanding treatment, but needs security and comfort with herself before she can give up her unhealthy attitudes.

THINGS OUR FEELINGS TEACH US

What our feelings teach us leaves us with opinions about ourselves. Our feelings about experiences give us a "felt way of life." As what we learn by watching leaves a "parent" inside us, our early feelings leave a "little child" inside us.

How Feelings Affect Our Reactions

How people react to a child affects her feelings about herself. Being told she is a "good little girl" makes her happy and pleased with herself. Being shamed or scolded leaves her feeling dirty, bad, or wrong. Remember (Chapter 1) how feelings get associated with other people, things, places, and events. Different parents praise and blame children for different ways of acting. So some people feel good about themselves for different things than other people do—and the same is true about bad feelings.

Report cards always gave Jodi a "funny feeling" in the stomach. Her brother always got praised for good grades. Her grades were good, too, and she felt that something must be wrong about this since she was not also praised. She overheard her mother tell a friend, "Jodi's a funny little girl; she would rather read than fuss around in the kitchen with me." So, although success makes many people feel good about themselves, Jodi feels like something is not quite right about it and her.

Three Different "Me's." Psychiatrist Harry Stack Sullivan said that how others react to us when we are children leaves us with three different me's. "Good-me" stands for the things that drew positive reactions. When we do these things we feel good about ourselves; sometimes if we don't do them, we feel bad about ourselves. Gen is never without a smile. As a child she was praised for her sunshiny disposition, and ignored when she was unhappy or out of sorts. Gen feels good about herself only when acting as if she is happy.

When we do things that cause bad reactions from others, we get anxious. "Bad-me" leaves us feeling as if something terrible is going to happen to us, and that we deserve it. Most people try to avoid situations with bad-me feelings. Often this is not helpful. Kay remembers that whenever she expressed an opinion that differed from her parents', they called her "Miss Know-It-All." She quit expressing opinions. Although Kay knows now that she needs to develop her own ideas, she finds it less threatening to agree with others' opinions. When she plans to say what she thinks, she gets so nervous that she quickly gives up the idea.

The third me is "not-me." This refers to experiences so traumatic that we can't even let ourselves remember them, so we lie to ourselves about them. If a jealous child hit the baby, her parents might react with such outrage that she becomes unable to let herself feel jealousy. As an adult, she may act so jealously that people can see it, but she is unable to see it herself. For some people, others' reactions to early sexual experimentation were so traumatic that they deny their sexual feelings.

The "Not-Okay" Child. Thus, everyone has a not-okay child in them that gets triggered by some events. Someone else's meaningless action or a small thing someone says—not even intended for us—can trip us into feeling not-okay. Good friends know what "hooks" each other, and learn either to avoid these things out of the friendship or to use them when they want to "get" the other. When you see pouting, sulking, crying, or temper tantrums, someone's not-okay child is at work.

We can do much to understand bad feelings about ourselves. When feeling not-okay, try to recall what was happening when the feelings started. Making notes for yourself will help you see the patterns in your bad feelings about yourself. Such self-understanding helps you understand others who feel bad about themselves and become hard to deal with. Some common situations that make women have not-okay feelings are listed in Box 2.1. (We will talk about how to work with unhelpful feelings in Chapter 5.)

Be careful not to blame your parents for too much about your early life. Parents differ in skills and knowledge for rearing children. They also differ in their own integration, harmful experiences, and handicaps in dealing with others. Everyone has some bad-me reactions; this is part of being a human being. Honest women will admit to bad-me feelings in some of the situations in Box 2.1. Many common cultural expectations set us up for this.

SOME PARTICULAR BAD FEELINGS

When we act against our values and morals we may feel very unhappy about it. Regret and sorrow are common, and sometimes we also feel disgust that values have been violated. These helpful feelings motivate us to get our behavior back in line with our values.

Some other reactions are not so helpful. They leave us

BOX 2.1
TRIGGERS FOR "NOT-OKAY" FEELINGS

having an important success
winning in competition with someone else
having someone turn down your invitation
seeing your good friend have fun with someone else
not being invited to an event to which your friends are invited
turning down someone who asks for a favor
having another person be angry with you
being angry with someone else
declining to do volunteer work you were asked to do
having more of something than someone else
getting a more choice part of a shared meal, excursion, or other event
having someone you know succeed more than you did
seeing others' successes in work, marriage, etc.
being alone on important holidays
having others report your child's misbehavior
having your choices win out over others'
giving your opinions when they differ from others'
having a member of your family make a social goof
not meeting someone else's expectations
being excluded from something because of your gender, race,
    religion, ethnicity, etc.
having others treat you more nicely than you expected
asserting your rights, desires, or preferences
outshining a man in any way
being loved by someone you consider very superior to yourself
being treated with deference
ending a love relationship
having troubles in a love relationship or friendship
having the neighbors overhear a family fight
disagreeing with someone else
making a complaint about poor goods or services you have bought
having someone see your house or office in a messy condition
not understanding what others are talking about, or saying some-
    thing "stupid"
disliking someone else

caught in bad feelings about ourselves, and may paralyze us from action. Often they make it even more likely that we will not respect ourselves enough to make needed changes. Although such feelings may come from bad behavior, they often come from our not-okay child and have nothing to do with real values.

Shame. When ashamed, you feel looked at, exposed, and vulnerable. You want to sink into the ground and disappear. Your face feels very hot, and you blush. Erik Erikson says shame is a "visual" experience, feeling like you are standing "naked" in front of other people.

Shame is usually concerned with fear of how others will react to you. The key to shame is thinking that others will "find out" or "see" something about you. Some people become ashamed so easily that they fear others will realize that they have common human limitations and weaknesses. People can be ashamed of bodily processes, too. Judy always flushes the toilet before she urinates in a public bathroom; she is ashamed to have anyone hear her.

A person's first response to shame is secrecy. She tries to hide, as Judy does behind the sound of the flushing toilet. Ashamed people may cut themselves off from other people. They also want reassurance that they are okay, and the more they withdraw, the harder getting it is. The Japanese suicidal practice of hara-kiri is an extreme way to "save face" when one cannot see a way out of a shameful situation.

Loni told me about her shame when she was excluded from a religious service because she is a woman. A male friend invited her to a non-Christian worship. When they went in, men were already standing in a line waiting to begin. Her friend stood next to the last man, and she at the end. She wondered why a few men who came in later went to the other end of the line. At first, she went through all the service movements with the men. Then the leader passed out a prayer sheet. After giving one to her friend, he went back to the front of the group. Loni then realized that they were treating her as if she were not even there. Her face burned, and she longed to be out of there—anywhere so long as it was out! She felt awkward, dirty, and bad. She was afraid to keep performing the service, and afraid to walk to the door and leave. She just wanted to disappear. It was one of her worst experiences.

People differ in how easily they feel shame. Having been shamed early in life makes you more susceptible. Fear of shame can keep you from doing things; the threat of humiliation controls your behavior. Avoiding something out of shame has nothing to do with being moral, of course. It can even work against moral behavior when that brings bad reactions from others. People shamed beyond endurance often become defiant and shameless. They may try to get away with whatever they can so long as they are not found out. Such shameless people do not need more shaming. Your own experiences of shame can help you understand them.

Self-Doubt. Self-doubting people are unsure of their adequacy and acceptability. A doubting person is less concerned with what others think than with how what they think makes her feel about herself. We can doubt ourselves if caught in an unworthy action, but also just by awareness of our ability to act badly. These things may have no moral content. A self-doubter worries about what she has "left behind" that shows unworthiness or failure. She worries about work others see, how she acted in social situations, whether she said the right thing, how her house and clothing look—anything others can use to evaluate her. She then takes negative reactions as showing her lack of worth.

Deb frequently has a common experience of self-doubters. When a group break up in laughter after she leaves them, she immediately wonders what about her they are ridiculing. She does not think that someone might have told a joke, or of any other reasons for the laughter. Her immediate belief is that she made some stupid mistake or acted inappropriately, and that they are making fun of her.

Other self-doubters are afraid to finish tasks for fear they won't measure up to someone else's standards. They put off work, and are afraid to "let go" and have fun in social situations. Unless others respond enthusiastically to them, they feel like complete failures. Often, if they get approval, they think others are mistaken or don't really know them. Thus, they never are comfortable dealing with other people. Some self-doubting women overdress or wear too much makeup to hide their insecurity. Some make themselves very dowdy hoping to pass unnoticed so that no one will comment on them at all. When you must deal with a procrastinator or a shrinking violet, she probably has a lot of self-doubt.

Guilt. Guilt is an "auditory" experience—that nagging inner voice that accuses and scolds you. Here nobody else feeds you bad feelings; you talk yourself into them. When someone unknowingly hooks your not-okay child, the result is often guilt—even though the other has not judged you in any way. Feeling guilty is different from an objective assessment of having done something wrong. Guilt ties you up in knots and makes you despise yourself. It doesn't produce reasonable plans about future behavior.

Joelle was very busy with many minor family crises. When she was asked to donate for a bake sale, she flared up in anger and yelled that they should ask someone who sits around doing nothing. Later she could not understand what came over her. Joelle's reaction is very common in people who easily feel guilt. She was taught always to be helpful and to pull her fair share. She usually was overworked because she felt guilty if she ever refused to help. Eventually the demands on her became so heavy that she got resentful, although she wasn't aware of it. She felt used and abused. She resented people who did less than she did because they still felt good about themselves. Being asked to donate to the bake sale was the last straw. Her anger was a desperate cry for help. Joelle took many months to learn that she need not feel guilty about caring for herself also, and that she had a right to say no to some requests.

Guilty people usually watch themselves very carefully, and try to control feelings or thoughts they think they should not have. They usually do not realize their "real" guilt—their inability to love themselves and others. Sometimes confession, voluntarily shaming themselves before another, relieves guilt. They may punish themselves—sometimes not knowing they are doing so—for unimportant failures. Sometimes they deprive themselves of small comforts and satisfactions. Often they choose unhelpful self-punishments. Depression is very common among guilty people. Some commit suicide—an extreme self-punishment. Anyone who often feels bad, depressed, or evil has disturbed guilt reactions.

Some guilty people become very moralistic as their unrecognized anger grows. They condemn people who do what they consider sinful, and sometimes go out of their way to make trouble for them. They may defend their cruelty with scriptures or moral principles that "prove" that the others deserve harsh treatment. A strongly moralistic person is usually extremely hard on herself, angry because she can't love herself, and takes her anger out on people who are easier on themselves.

Understanding her bad feelings about herself helps you deal with her.

DELUSIONS

Delusions are beliefs that are not true, which cannot be corrected by reasoning. They differ from mistakes about facts, which we all make, by being motivated by feelings. Delusions occur when strong feelings color our perceptions of the world, ourselves, and other people. Recall Deb's feeling that she was judged negatively by people. Delusions lead us to do things that mess up situations. We act from misperceptions that make us expect negative responses from others. Acting thus, we tend to get the very reactions that confirm our worst fears.

Laura was quite sure that her colleagues rejected her ideas because of prejudice against women. She became more and more insistent that, if they were open-minded, they would see things as she did. As her demands increased, they withdrew from her, and discounted her ideas before she had even completely expressed them. Laura felt confirmed in her belief that they had pre-judged her. Because of her delusion, she failed to ask for feedback about why they disliked her ideas. With it, she might have been able to rethink her proposals to make them workable. Instead, she became even more deeply entrenched in her negative expectations.

Someone who consistently draws frustrating responses from others may be setting herself up for them. If you can figure out what expectations she is confirming, you may be able to stop her destructive behavior. Making someone see her delusions is hard, but you may help by not confirming them. Refuse to play her destructive "game."

HOW EXPECTATIONS AND FEELINGS LAST

You have seen how our observations and feelings leave us with differing expectations about life, ourselves, and others, and some ways we maintain these expectations. We now look at other understandings about how these ideas last, and at some self-perceptions that they give us.

Maintaining a Worldview

Alfred Adler said that early in life we develop a "guiding fiction." He called it a fiction because this worldview comes from our own limited experiences, which are only a small part of all human experience. Since we would need all possible experiences for full understanding, our limited views are bound to contain fictions we have created. Although our observations and feelings lay the basis for our guiding fiction, we also actively form it.

Attribution. We all try to understand our experiences, make them meaningful, and interpret them. Attributions, the causes we use to explain our experiences, usually refer either to personal characteristics (our own or others') or to external circumstances. Our attributions help form our guiding fiction.

Tina is very overweight. She fears rejection from others, and avoids many social situations. Tina sees her weight as the cause of her troubles. If she doesn't lose weight, she can continue to believe that all her problems will be solved if (when) she does. Tina explains problems by one characteristic of hers—and life is seldom that simple. Recall that Laura did similarly; she blamed her work difficulties on one presumed characteristic of her co-workers.

Marie, who is very bright, grew up believing that she

had no abilities. An older sister's accomplishments always outshone hers. When Marie began having important successes in college, she could not accept her own role in producing them. She attributed them all to the kindness of her professors or to luck. Thus she explained her outcomes by external factors.

When people explain outcomes by one person's characteristics or by a simple understanding of the environment, it helps them make sense of puzzling events, but seldom does justice to the complexity of situations. Once we make such attributions, seeing evidence confirming them is easier than seeing denying evidence. When we can explain events in several possible ways, we tend to choose those consistent with the guiding fiction because it is our frame of reference for all that happens. Because of its importance, we do not easily change inadequate understandings for better ones.

Cognitive Dissonance. Sometimes our understandings get jarred enough to make us uneasy. We also feel this cognitive dissonance when our attitudes and our behavior do not fit together well. Dissonance occurs when the parts of our psychological life are not in harmony.

Kathy chain-smokes. As the health warnings about smoking became more publicized, Kathy kept saying that maybe she should quit. However, she never did. Then Kathy stopped talking about quitting and seemed comfortable with her smoking. Occasionally, when pressed about it, she said that she knows she should quit, but that her life is too pressured to do it right now.

This shows how cognitive dissonance works. It makes us uneasy. When it is present, something has to go— either a belief that doesn't fit with other important beliefs or behavior or else a behavior that doesn't fit. To hold on to both dissonant things is too uncomfortable. Kathy's first thought was to quit smoking, but she was unable to do so. Then she ignored the health warnings (making those beliefs "not there" for herself) so she could comfortably smoke. When she was made to look at these warnings, she convinced herself that she would quit eventually. She used several ways to deal with cognitive dissonance.

Two other ways to deal with dissonance are the "sour grapes" and "sweet lemon" reactions. You try to convince yourself that you did not really want what you cannot have, or that you really like something you didn't want but with which you are stuck. You also may try to get others to agree with important particular beliefs to bolster your own faltering belief. Marge told me that she never defended her religious beliefs more strongly than when she was least sure of them.

Worldview Rigidity. Attribution and cognitive dissonance show us how hard it is to change set ways of understanding life—ways developed from observing and reacting to early life experiences. Cognitive dissonance helps us understand why people who feel threatened or insecure become dogmatic and insist that others see and do things their way.

We all carry on an inner conversation with ourselves, rehearsing the worldview that determines our actions. You can learn your rigid and unyielding places by tuning in on that inner conversation. A later chapter tells you how to modify it. You can also develop sympathy for others' rigidities by realizing that they, like you, try to make sense of their lives, develop consistent understandings, and protect what they think they understand.

SOME WORLDVIEW EFFECTS ON SELF-UNDERSTANDING

Part of our worldview is the relatively lasting pictures we develop of ourselves. We now look at several that are difficult to change and on which people differ greatly.

Competence. All people want to be effective, do things well, and deal with life. We get impressions of our general competence from how others react to us. These ideas commonly determine whether we will even try to deal with certain situations, and how long we will keep trying if we do.

Some people get accurate opinions of their competence, but others' experiences leave them with distorted ideas. They have often learned to be helpless. Such people usually cannot recognize when situations change, and when circumstances that might once have kept them genuinely helpless are no longer present. Many women who have been abused have learned to be helpless. People who feel helpless usually become passive, apathetic, and depressed.

It is hardest to change a person's feelings of helplessness when she believes that the conditions for it are (1) permanent and cannot be changed, (2) part of her personality instead of the environment, and (3) affecting much of her functioning instead of a small part of it. Once she is convinced of her lack of competence, others' reassurances do not help her change. Neither does observing others make mistakes or have failures. The best way to improve her opinion about her abilities is actually to engage her in successful action. Giving her tasks within her abilities can effectively improve her opinion of herself and alleviate doubts about competence.

Locus of Control. A similar self-opinion concerns how much control we think our action has over outcomes. Some competent people believe that forces outside them determine their outcomes. Julian Rotter classified people as internals or externals, depending on whether they thought their outcomes were shaped by their own actions or by forces outside their control.

Internals much more successfully manage their lives, control their habits, and deal with other people. Unfortunately, some people's life experiences leave them feeling less in control than others. Usually more intelligent, highly educated, and higher social class people feel stronger internal control. Men are more internal than women. Less privileged people—women and others with fewer advantages—might simply have learned that they do, indeed, have less control over their outcomes than more privileged people.

This creates special problems for women. Little girls have often been taught that their rewards in life will come from having some man responsible for them. The media support this impression, with magazine and television stories showing men producing their own outcomes and women being given them by men acting on their behalf. Also, women often are discriminated against in ways that make it more difficult, or even impossible, to obtain certain outcomes. Sadly, even within their churches, women often are denied opportunities for certain ministries, or these are made much more difficult for them. We need, however, to encourage ourselves and other women to take responsibility for whatever outcomes we can. The improved self-functioning that goes with an internal control orientation is worth the difficulties involved in working for it.

Self-Esteem. Self-esteem is the valuation we put on ourselves. We differ widely in how highly we value ourselves. The emotions we easily experience, how competent we perceive ourselves to be, and how much we feel in control of our lives all feed into our evaluation of personal worth. These color our expectations, affect how we act, and help determine our resultant opinion of ourselves.

This important characteristic of self-esteem will be discussed more in later chapters. We next look at some different types of adult people that are produced by the forces working on us during our formative years.

CHAPTER 3

Some Different Kinds of People

Variety's the very spice of life.
—William Cowper,
The Task II

This chapter looks at two major ways in which people differ. First, they reach different levels of individual maturity. People of the same age vary greatly in their psychological integration and maturity. Second, people develop important stylistic differences in how they think and do things, regardless of how mature they are.

PERSONAL MATURITY

Many kinds of maturity have been studied: physical, intellectual, psychosocial, moral, ego, and faith. We focus here on ego development since it summarizes many aspects of personal psychological growth. Speaking of maturity recognizes that some people seem never to grow up, while others achieve adult and effective ways of managing their lives.

How Ego Development Works

Some development, such as physical and intellectual, is tied very strongly to chronological age. With others, such as ego, moral, or faith development, a minimum age seems necessary for some levels of maturity, but age is no guarantee of continuing to develop.

We can describe stages of development. A person cannot move to a higher stage until the one just before it is satisfactorily managed. Each stage builds on the stages before it, and lays the foundation for the next one. All the stages occur in a fixed order. No one can skip a stage, but people move through the stages at different speeds. People look different at each stage. Some traits that you have in lower stages disappear as you mature. Some new traits appear only at higher levels of development. For example, as people mature they usually become less impulsive and more able to see issues from many different sides.

Since people develop at different speeds, and vary in motivation and opportunities for maturing, not all people reach the higher stages. Each stage will be the last for some people. Sometimes people stuck at one stage start developing again later in life, and move up a stage or more. No one ever gets too old for more personal maturity.

You will surely recognize people you know who fit into some of these stages. Some will fall between two stages, with features of each. You may be tempted to figure out where you fall in them. Since we can understand one or two stages higher than our own, you might think you are farther along than you are. Be careful if you try to decide where you fit; most people overrate themselves.

JANE LOEVINGER'S EGO DEVELOPMENT MODEL

A developmental model describes changes people go through as they mature. Jane Loevinger saw four major parts in ego development: (1) morality, and how we manage impulses; (2) how we deal with other people; (3) what kinds of things are on our mind; and (4) our style of understanding ourselves, life, and other people.

Moral Style. As they grow older, children learn to control their impulses better and begin to understand moral rules and fair play. Such growth need not end in childhood; it can get more and more refined throughout life. From being very undercontrolled and impulse-ridden, with no concern for others, people can develop moral values that they have thought hard about, prayed over, and tried to run their lives by. Yet some adults look like little children in how they manage themselves. They have not learned to say no to themselves regarding anything they want. You worry about what they will do if somebody isn't around to watch them. Loevinger traces the process we go through in moral maturing. She describes how impulse control and morality look at each stage.

Interpersonal Style. Interpersonal style is about how you treat people and expect people to treat you. Adults, just like children, differ in how they manage relationships. Some people give very little, but expect to get whatever they want from others. Some use temper tantrums to get their own way, or pout or withdraw when things don't please them. Some try to manipulate or "use" others. Still others highly respect people and treat them as they would like to be treated themselves. As with moral style, we follow a certain path to maturity in handling relationships. Loevinger's stages describe this growth.

Conscious Preoccupations and Cognitive Style. Our conscious preoccupations are what we find ourselves thinking about. When you don't have to attend to other things, your mind keeps going back to certain things. Loevinger believes these say a lot about your maturity. With personal growth, definite changes occur in what keeps running through your mind.

Cognitive style is the hardest aspect of ego development to understand. Little children see things only from a very simple perspective. They need very easy understandings, and even distort facts to make them look simple when things get too complicated. Some adults do not outgrow simplistic answers and easy solutions. As with the other aspects of ego development, changes take place in both preoccupations and cognitive style with increasing maturity.

THE LEVELS OF EGO DEVELOPMENT

We do not describe Loevinger's lower (Autistic and Symbiotic) levels and very highest (Integrated) stage of ego development because so few people fit them.

Impulse-ridden Stage. Kelly worries about morals only when she may be caught or get in trouble. She seems not to understand that people need rules of conduct to live together. For her, the only bad action is one that is punished. Kelly lives by her impulses; she gets drunk at times and is considered "easy" sexually.

When Kelly is frustrated or upset, she has a temper tantrum. She sees other people as sources of supply, and judges them by how much they give her. In her self-centeredness, she disregards others' feelings and wishes. If interpersonal problems get too big, she runs away from the situation.

Kelly spends most of her time thinking about what she wants and what she feels like doing. When things are not exciting, she is bored and tries to stir up some excitement. She sees responsibilities as burdens. She doesn't realize that she causes most of her problems, but typically blames other people and situations. She said, "I don't have a drinking problem; the trouble is that I have to pass a bar on the way home from work."

Expectedly, Kelly finds it hard to keep a job or friends,

and her life is chaotic. The few grown women at this low level of maturity are often in trouble with the law. People who must deal with them quickly learn that they cannot be relied upon or trusted. The best way to manage a Kelly is to expect little from her, and to refuse to be mistreated by her.

Self-protective Stage. Mattie's chief rule is "Don't get caught." She can control impulses better than Kelly, and does so when it's to her advantage. Mattie understands moral rules, and bends them to her purposes. "What's in it for me?" is her chief consideration in deciding what to do.

Mattie divides other people into two groups: those who control her and those whom she can control. She wants control, and tries to avoid those who control her. People she does not like pay for it. She easily feels mistreated, and makes sure to "get even" whenever she can. She is smart enough to take her revenge carefully and not get in trouble.

Mattie thinks a lot about how to avoid work, look for fun, and get plenty of life's good things like money. She feels that whatever anyone else gains, she somehow loses. She gets sad about others' successes and happiness, and feels cheated. She likes hostile humor, and holds grossly prejudiced and stereotyped pictures of other people. Mattie often sees herself as a pawn of fate. Her search for the easy way out leaves her failing to understand much of life's complexity.

There are more Matties around than you might think. Mattie has social poise, and has learned to "look good" to get away with manipulating people and situations. How to deal with Mattie? You can convince her that your plans and ideas will work to her advantage. You can also refuse to be taken in by her manipulations. Do not expect much group spirit or cooperative effort from her.

Conformist Stage. Like Edith, many people end up at the conformist stage. Edith "buys" authority completely, and obeys the rules simply because they are the rules. She judges her own and other people's actions by their conformity to traditional standards of right and wrong, and she applies these rules rigidly. She sees a right and wrong way to act in every situation, at all times, for all people—with no exceptions. Edith gets upset when people disregard conventional gender and social roles; she thinks women should be women, men should be men, and all should know their own place. Edith very carefully behaves properly herself.

Edith needs people to like her and approve of her. She is greatly controlled by what others think because disapproval upsets her greatly. She likes to consider everyone her friend, and will not say unkind things about anyone—except "sinners." Good manners are also important, and Edith is careful not to show anger or displeasure because people should always be nice. Tension in one of her groups makes Edith very uncomfortable, and she tries to smooth things over.

Edith thinks a lot about what people think of her. Keeping up with others in style, clothes, prestige, property, etc., is very important. She is ashamed of a house not picked up, clothes not ironed, or an out-of-date dress or car. She is also very sentimental, and saves mementos from high school and college. She remembers only the good points of dead family and friends. She thinks that love and marriage always go together, and that love and sex are opposites in many ways. Edith sees life very simply. She says she doesn't have any inner conflicts, and thinks all problems can be solved easily if people only act as they should.

You probably know many Ediths. They don't cause much trouble because getting along with others and being liked is so important to them. However, getting them to give honest opinions is difficult because they don't let themselves recognize their uncomfortable feelings. Ediths are not likely to be creative because they fear new ideas. An Edith needs lots of encouragement to help her understand that it's okay to differ from others.

Self-aware Level. By high school age some people move to self-awareness. This comes much later for others. Joan is a latecomer to self-awareness after many years as a good conformist. When she started questioning the rules, she decided that circumstances can affect what is the right way to behave. She concluded that using the rules as guidelines is good, but she must decide if the rules really hold in her situations. Sometimes she feels guilty when she decides against accepted rules. She admits she may be morally confused, but knows she could never go back to simply applying rules without question.

Joan is self-conscious around other people. She is aware that she doesn't "fit" as perfectly as she had once thought, and is sensitive to her uniqueness. She sometimes wonders if she is not weird or strange. People are important to her, and she tries to be helpful to others, but she wants deeper and more honest relationships than she has had so far. She has tried encounter groups to learn new ways to interact with others.

Joan thinks about who she is, trying to understand herself as more than just a member of certain groups: family, church, neighborhood. She is starting to pay attention to her feelings, and suffers some inner conflict and turmoil. She views herself as changing, not as a finished product as she had viewed herself before. She sees many more possibilities in life than she had ever considered possible. She is also strongly aware of many differences among people she had not noticed before.

Joan's level of development is the most common for adults; conformist is second most common. Her self-awareness leaves her with many unanswered questions and concerns about herself. Sometimes retreating back to being conformist would be more comfortable, but she cannot make it work. Joan is caught at an uncomfortable level of development; she is unable to go backward and she finds it painful to progress. She needs support and sympathetic encouragement to continue discovering her own unique values and vocation.

Conscientious Stage. Conscientious development is almost impossible before early adulthood; many people never get this far. Becca's morality is much less based on rules. She decides on behavior by looking at her motives and the likely outcomes. She has defined her values and ideals through hard and painful effort. She is critical of herself regarding how well she keeps them, and hard on herself for her failures. She has a real conscience—standards that she has made part of herself—instead of simply doing as others tell her to do.

Becca thinks of her relationships in terms of the ideals and feelings of the people involved; a friend is someone who shares her goals and values, not just someone with whom she goes bowling or to the movies. Becca is a very loyal and responsible friend; people can count on her. Sometimes she gets overprotective of others. Becca feels so strongly about her own hard-won insights that she considers sharing them a favor, and may try to impose them on others. She doesn't want others to conform to her, but to recognize the values she appreciates.

Becca is much more concerned with self-respect than with what others think of her. Living properly is her major preoccupation. She very highly values achievement, considering it important to use her abilities and talents. For her, not to develop herself fully would be wrong. She ponders her motives and personal characteristics since self-understanding is also an important value.

Becca is aware of life's complexity, and tries to find patterns of meaning for her own understanding. She refuses to oversimplify things, though, and realizes that she must live without firm answers to some questions.

Having a Becca around is usually a joy. She often winds up in leadership positions. She is diligent and responsible, and you can count on her to follow through on duties and commitments. She may be somewhat overconvinced about the merits of her own ideas, but usually she will accept solutions that are fair to all concerned.

Individualistic Level. Even fewer people become individualistic. Simone's understanding of her own ethic is very clear, but sometimes she questions which claims should take priority over others. In Simone, some of Becca's excessive responsibility for others has given way to increased willingness to let others have different values without her feeling a need to educate or correct them. Her relationships with others are very important to her, and she works on keeping them free of inappropriate dependence and expectations.

Simone is very aware of her emotional states and internal conflicts. Social problems and total personal development now concern her more than simple achievement. She involves herself in service roles in community affairs, and does not demand particular outcomes. She does things that she thinks worth doing and, after doing her best, does not fret about results. She does not mind living with insecurity, paradoxes, and apparent contradictions in life. One need not worry about getting along with a Simone. She deals with her own problems adequately enough that issues don't spill over into relationships.

Autonomous Stage. Not much can be said about the autonomous stage since few people get this far. Here impulse control is no longer a problem, and all moral concern is about priorities and appropriateness, such as balancing duties, rights, and obligations. This person knows and deals well with her inner conflicts. She has a great respect for individuality, and lets others choose their own paths and make their own mistakes. However, she cherishes personal ties. She holds broad social ideals and understands herself in a social context. The autonomous person can tie together apparently incompatible ideas and alternatives.

Mothering and Level of Development. A summary of the major ego development stages is seen in how a mother might act at these stages. The impulsive mother does not really mother at all; she is too busy satisfying her own needs. A self-protective mother teaches her child to "look out for number one." Conformist mothers are very concerned with "what will the neighbors think?" and demand politeness and conformity. Conscientious mothers want their children to follow the guiding philosophy that the mother developed for herself. An autonomous mother realizes that her children must live their own lives; she gives example, guidance, and—when asked for it—advice, but does not try to "mold" her child as many other mothers do.

DIFFERENCES IN PERSONAL STYLE

Regardless of maturity, people differ in other important ways. People of the same maturity do not all have the same stylistic features, although some styles "fit" better with different levels of maturity. A person's style stays with her, to some extent, through all levels of maturity. It may be cruder at lower levels and become more refined as she develops. A style may be manifest in full-blown fashion—as in our examples that follow—or in a less exaggerated way. Interpersonal problems are most likely when people have very different styles.

COMPULSIVES AND IMPULSIVES

Eve strongly needs to do things in a precise, exact way. People often see her as rigid because of her set routines. She keeps her things very tidy, and organizes her time tightly. Often she knows in good detail exactly how she will spend each day weeks in advance. Eve takes longer at tasks than many people because she pays close attention to small details to make sure she is working carefully. Eve has trouble "letting go" and playing. She is uncomfortable in situations that aren't highly structured. Interruptions and people who misplace things greatly annoy her. Eve suffers unhelpful guilt (Chapter 2); she cannot feel "right" unless constantly proving her worth by hard work, productivity, and service.

Eve will usually be more comfortable with "behind the scenes" detailed work. She is a good choice for managing money and accounting, arranging plans and assignments, and developing workable timetables. If a job requires close attention and patient perseverance, Eve will do it well. Be careful not to pressure her; she already feels pressured. If she procrastinates because she thinks her efforts are not good enough, notice and thank her for little achievements. Don't let Eve stay behind to "finish up" when others are leaving a task. Encourage her to play with you; tell her that you have a right to some of her company! Be cheerful and openly friendly with her, especially when she is *not* being productive. Try not to rebuff her, as she suffers much self-doubt.

Shari is the opposite of Eve in many ways. She acts on the spur of the moment most of the time. When an idea hits her, it is often in action before it has even been thought through. Shari doesn't plan in advance, and often seems thoughtless about obligations and commitments. She may leave projects half finished if another idea hits her. Shari often has good insights, and may find creative solutions to thorny situations. She also can be a lot of fun, and put a spirit of lightness into heavy problems.

Shari needs quite different management from Eve. Don't make her responsible for a task if it will mess things up if she doesn't come through. Give Shari deadlines—for making a choice, for finishing a project—earlier than when you really need action. Let her know your displeasure openly when she misses a deadline. She needs to know how she causes trouble for others. Be sure, of course, to focus on the current problem; don't drag in old history or catalog everything wrong with her. When you need to open up a wide range of options, ask Shari to brainstorm ideas. If you have trouble relaxing and playing, be sure to go along with some of her spontaneous suggestions: "Wouldn't it be fun to take off and go to the beach now?" Shari needs to learn when her impulsiveness is a problem, and when it is a helpful love of the fullness of life.

CONTROLLERS AND YIELDERS

Gwen feels insecure when not in control of situations. She is apt to seize power whenever she can, and to rule with an iron fist. Others must pay attention to what Gwen wants, when she wants them to. Every issue is important for her. She becomes very impatient when others fail to "cooperate." She uses many tactics—ridicule, anger, resistance—to bring people to her positions. Gwen forces others to agree with her because she knows no other style of relating to them.

The best way to deal with Gwen is to show her that two heads are better than one. Avoid a head-on fight with her. Never back her into a corner or cause her to lose face if you want to continue relating to her. When she tries overhard to coerce you, react with passivity until she runs out of steam. In a low-keyed way, then note the good points in what she said and also where you disagree with her. Don't let her get into lengthy reexplanations. Tell her you think you understand her, and will let her ask you questions to be sure you do. The key ideas are to be calm, persistent, and supportive while refusing to yield all control.

Micky agrees with everything proposed. Because rejection terrifies her more than anything else, she says what she thinks others want to hear. She dares not express a counteropinion for fear of conflict. Unfortunately, Micky's mouth is more active than the rest of her. She makes promises, agrees with proposals, and commits herself to things that she cannot follow through on. Sometimes she is overwhelmed by the sheer number of promises she has made.

Micky must be encouraged to be more honest. Don't accept a simple "yes" from her. Get her to elaborate her ideas, especially those which differ from others' opinions. Ask her to criticize proposed plans, and don't let her get away without comment. Then praise her honesty and good input. If she makes a commitment, agree on a timetable and specific details of what is promised. Appreciate her independent thought and action, insist on follow-through on commitments, and don't feel obligated by her agreeableness.

PRACTICALS AND ROMANTICS

Amy prides herself on being practical. She knows the likely outcomes and rewards of any action before she commits herself to it. She doesn't trust her impulses, and works everything over, again and again, in her head. Feelings are pushed out of awareness as she analyzes situations for measurable outcomes. Amy doesn't trust the satisfactions that come from emotional involvements, and evaluates interpersonal relationships only in terms of gains and payoffs. She seeks above all to avoid being hurt or disappointed. Trish says she can see the calculator going in Amy's head when she considers whether or not to get involved in any way.

Amy is difficult to deal with since she doesn't trust. Be aware of how vulnerable she is, and be absolutely trustworthy with her. Changing plans you have made or begging off a commitment leaves her confirmed in needing to protect herself from others' fickleness. Share with her how you have put your own emotional hurts in perspective. If you yourself believe it, let her know that you consider the gains from emotional investments worth the costs. Refuse to cooperate in her pragmatic assessments when they do not feel "right" to you, and tell her why.

Carol is also continually disappointed by people. However, she is easily attracted to others and considers each new attraction the biggest "find" of her life. She gets so caught up in her feelings that she sees only good in others, and refuses to recognize relationship tensions. She is patient, kind, and unwilling to take back any commitment she has made, believing that ultimately trusting love will cure all ills. No matter how badly a person may treat her, she is always ready for more. Repeatedly, she is abandoned by people on whom she poured out her love. Although she persists in optimism that others will appreciate her, she is becoming increasingly unsure of her own lovableness. She still makes excessive attempts to win others over. Carol never objectively assesses other people, her relationships, or her life. She insists on remaining naive, and acting on her feelings, no matter how much she is misused.

Carol is also a difficult problem. If she has attached herself to you, don't let her become a martyr for you.

Refuse to take advantage of her willingness. If you feel bad because you are not as invested in her as she is in you, discuss it with her. Let her know of your discomfort, and that you need to discuss the boundaries of the relationship. Get her to tell you her wishes, support her right to them, and be frank about which you can or want to meet. If she wants more time and energy than you want to give her, tell her the limits of your willingness so that you can decide together if a relationship is possible. Stick to your own position. If she finds it unacceptable, tell her that you don't think she likes the person you really are since you want more time for other things besides her. If Carol has attached herself to men in a martyr fashion, help her see their flaws by asking her to talk about what bothers her about them. Encourage her to discuss her expectations with them so they can let her know if their plans match her hopes or not.

ATTACKERS AND WITHDRAWERS

Gina frequently vents her rage against other people. If complaining does not make them miserable enough, she resorts to other tactics. Her clever verbal barbs leave others hurt or confused. Sometimes her potshots strike at particular targets, and sometimes she seems out to "get" everyone. She seldom has anything good to say about anyone else. She is very sensitive to others' flaws, and talks about them to anyone who will listen. She draws other people into arguments, and seems so full of anger that there is room for nothing else. Others usually feel uncomfortable in her presence.

Behind almost every anger, you find an afraid or hurting person. Since anger is easier to feel than hurt or fear, some people settle into chronic hostility. If Gina intimidates you, you are not the right person to deal with her. She must be managed with calmness, courtesy, courage, and firmness. Offer sympathy for her bad feelings without blaming yourself or anyone else. Acknowledge her complaints, then insist on discussing a solution. Don't listen to repeated similar complaints until she makes progress toward solving the problem. Don't listen to complaints about another's character; listen to complaints only about specific problems. Tell her that you don't feel able to judge others, and that they must speak for themselves. If Gina is speaking against you, refuse to retaliate, but do tell her—in private—that you don't like her behavior. Insist that she tell you her real problem with you, so that you can work with her to do something about it. Sometimes you can say to a Gina, "You seem to be hurting a lot." This may help her recognize buried feelings of hurt or fear.

Eileen draws back from others, keeping her thoughts and feelings to herself. People cannot get to know her; the wall she has built around herself seems impenetrable. Sometimes she seems shy and afraid to reach out; at other times, she seems to be on an angry sit-down strike. She refuses to discuss things or be involved, often to the point of exasperating others. She seldom asks for anything, and seems almost always silent and unresponsive.

Sometimes an Eileen needs permission to talk—especially if her social fear is high. Try to draw her out by asking her opinions. You can sometimes get her to talk more by picking up on a comment and asking for more information, for example: "You said things seem a bit crazy around here today. What did you have in mind?" Sometimes you can guess what she is feeling and say something like, "Your face looked so sad a minute ago." Then wait until she makes some reply. If it seems that Eileen is not really afraid to talk, but uses silence as a tactic, you might try to smoke her out. You can go silent yourself, when one-to-one, and wait until she responds; be prepared for the awkward discomfort of a long silence. Don't bail her out. If you must leave with nothing done, say so and ask something like, "How can we get this taken care of?" Sometimes an Eileen stays silent in a group until her silence gets attention focused on her. If this happens, get the group to refuse to play along with it. If it ceases to draw attention, Eileen will eventually give it up.

SHARPENERS AND BLUNTERS

Bev is acutely sensitive to her own and other people's distress. She hones in on bad feelings, worries a lot, and easily gets swamped by shame and guilt. Sometimes she feels the weight of the world on her shoulders, and holds herself responsible for righting things that she sees are wrong. She feels guilty because children are hungry, wars occur, and life is not harmonious. Bev's "misery threshold" is much lower than average, with a finely sharpened sense of negative emotions. Just being around her can leave you feeling "heavy."

Bev may need a therapist to dispel her misery. If she is suicidal, listen to her explain her despair without trying to talk her out of it. Then calmly tell her that you are going to help her find a professional who can help with her problems. If she is not dangerously depressed, but simply is chronically negative, you are best to ignore her misery in a group. If you reward such behavior with attention, she is encouraged to continue it. Voice positive feelings when you two are alone. If she says negative things, suggest other ways to look at them. Encourage her to write out her negative thoughts, and then think of other ways to look at them (see Chapter 5). Invite her to have fun with you, and refuse to let her dampen your spirits. Openly appreciate any positive reactions she has.

Faith blunts her awareness of bad feelings, shrugs off misery, refuses to acknowledge pain and sorrow, and looks on the bright side of every problem. She pays attention only to happy and joyful things, and insists on emphasizing the positive. She may chatter without stop, and act in excited and dramatic ways. Faith cannot stand a downcast face and insists on everybody's being happy. She refuses to look at difficult issues, deliberately blinding herself to problems to avoid having to deal with them.

Ordinarily, you probably like having Faith around. She lightens things up well. Be unresponsive to her exhibitionism if it drains you. When you must deal with a hard issue with her, lay out the facts as you see them and ask her to repeat what you said. Once she has clearly understood you, ask for her opinions. Refuse to accept shallow appeals to trust or love, and insist on an agreed-upon plan of action. Show appreciation for reflective comments that indicate her willingness to face hard realities. Let her know that she has your care and respect without having to be either a clown or a perpetual optimist.

CARETAKERS AND LEANERS

Helen moves naturally toward situations where she can caretake. She sees many around her as helpless or needing care, and attracts people who feel needy. Helen uses a caretaking tactic to draw others to her. She tries to become so indispensable that they cannot imagine doing without her. She willingly cares for others, protects them, and directs their lives—so long as they are docile and dependent. Not all her goodness is free, though! Since Helen needs to keep others tied to her, she may belittle them when they try to act independently. She keeps them needy by destroying their security about themselves. Sometimes, instead, she slightly changes others' dependence on her by becoming the person whose support and approval they need to try out new things. Once under Helen's wing, getting clear is hard.

Taking advantage of Helen would be easy. Her need to mother makes her prone to honor almost all requests.

You must be very careful with her lest she start feeling that she owns you. Insist on reciprocity in dealing with her; if she drove last time, you do it this time. Return favors scrupulously. Let her know that too much caretaking makes you uncomfortable. Encourage her to nurture herself. Be sure she knows that you accept her apart from what she does for you. In groups, don't let her become a workhorse. Surprise her occasionally with an unexpected favor.

Diane is a leaner. When she has a problem, her first question is, "Whom can I get to fix this?" She is talented at drawing others to her aid by looking helpless, appealing, and needy. Sometimes she emphasizes her own drawbacks to convince others of her need. Diane has no firm sense of her own personhood, and feels that her life would fall apart if she had no one to turn to. If she has trouble finding someone who will spend time with her, she cries about her loneliness, her sadness, or some invented crisis. She has even threatened suicide to keep others involved with her.

You must draw firm limits with a Diane so you will not be sucked dry. When she calls, explicitly tell her how long you can talk, and stick to it. If she claims a crisis, be sympathetic but firm about what involvement you can offer. If she threatens to fall apart or commit suicide, give her the name of a crisis center or a good therapist. When she asks for your advice and you give it, don't argue about it. Just say, "That's how I see it." If she doesn't follow your advice, refuse to give more, explaining that your advice doesn't seem helpful to her. Encourage her in every way you can when she handles things for herself. Ask her to do favors for you, and be grateful if she does. If she doesn't, tell her that your relationship doesn't seem to be mutual, and that you like to receive as well as give.

ABOUT DIFFERENT TYPES OF PEOPLE

Both the levels of maturity and the styles described will not fit any one person exactly. However, the more solidly a person is at one level of development, the more she will look like its description. The more extremely a person uses one adjustment style, the more she will look like the woman described with that style.

People at the extremes of any stylistic pair have the most trouble managing an appropriate relationship with each other. Some pairs would often disagree, and others would encourage each other in less adaptive ways of living. Probably you and the people you know look like you combine several styles and don't use any to the extreme. We tend to be composites of many different features.

Whenever someone uses one style to a problem extent, the management suggestions should be helpful, even though the person is not an extreme case. Less extreme people still have and cause trouble dealing with different others. Appreciating what people can contribute, while helping them moderate the more intense expressions of their style, is most helpful in producing satisfactory relationships.

We have really been talking about how to love people effectively, according to their real needs of character and personal growth. The next chapter looks at love and examines more ways to love ourselves and others truly, avoiding the pitfalls of faulty "love."

CHAPTER 4

Understanding How to Love

They do not love that do not show their love.
—Shakespeare,
The Two Gentlemen of Verona,
Act 1, Scene 2

Love, the major commandment of many world faiths, is poorly understood. The word itself is used in so many different ways that people discussing love often seem to be talking about very different things. This chapter tries to untangle some of the confusion.

PROBLEMS WITH THE WORD "LOVE"

Little agreement exists about what makes up love. The many different ideas about it sometimes fit poorly with each other. People also confuse issues of love and justice.

IDEAS ABOUT LOVE

Many psychologists consider love a need. Without it, we do not become fully human. Infants deprived of contact develop more slowly and have more severe health problems than others. Children reared in institutions are handicapped in establishing loving relations as they grow up.

Some people think of love as a contract—an idea that does not fit well with religious values. One bargains with another for payoffs. Each person tries to get the best value for what she can offer.

Others think love is feeling attracted to another person. For them, love is not possible without that feeling. If the feeling disappears, they decide that they no longer love.

For some, love is caring. You love another when you are concerned about her good. A sign of this concern is wanting to give to another, and caring about what happens to her.

Intimacy is love's key idea for other people. Love is the exchange between people of feelings, ideas, values, goals, and—sometimes—bodies.

Another view is that love is commitment. You promise to be "there" for a person you love. Honoring the promise is love. In this view, love is a decision on which you follow through.

Finally, some people consider love to be the creative energy that makes the universe function in harmony. Wherever it exists, it makes goodness, unifies persons, and unites people. It is like God's love for all creation.

All these understandings of love have some truth, yet each alone is limited. Some apply best to particular kinds of love. It is scant wonder that people get confused when they speak of love!

LOVE AND JUSTICE

Some people say that true justice would make love unnecessary. They see fair and equitable treatment of all persons as the most important need of human relationships. Some even think love makes justice impossible by singling out some people as more important than others.

Some love clearly requires a broad foundation of justice. Other loves have exclusiveness and selectivity as part of their meaning. These loves, such as friendship or romance, create positive good for people even though limited in their application. If conducted properly, they do not make fair treatment of others impossible.

Some other love-and-justice questions are about how

much to give people you love. Too much giving, or faulty giving, destroys both yourself and the other. A related question is when to "give up" on another. Although she may need love, or need her life "fixed" somehow, this responsibility is not always best seen as your own. Although such questions sound coldhearted, these very real issues must be considered.

TYPES OF LOVE

Our understanding increases when we "divide" love into different types. Box 4.1 describes some major ones. We now look at how they work. Two very important loves—self-love and love of neighbor (agape, pronounced ah-*gah*-pay)—are considered separately.

AFFECTION

Affection is a love for people nearest and dearest to you—usually family members and people like family. It grows out of physical closeness, and usually people cannot say exactly when it starts. You realize, "I've grown accustomed to her face . . ."

Affection is the love needed for human growth. Usually we get it from parents, and then give it back to them, sisters, brothers, and our children. Affection love is relaxed, courteous without need for "company manners." You can most easily be yourself when surrounded by affection. Unfortunately, some people push this too far, and are rude to those with whom they share affection.

Sometimes affection "eats up" a person. You become afraid to leave its comfort and security. Religions recognize that affection love can stunt growth (see Matt. 10:34ff.). To leave affection's security, sometimes you must give up your parents' cherished beliefs and practices; this may cost you their care. Religion might give one another family; "anyone who does the will of God is

BOX 4.1
TYPES OF LOVE

The Love	Person Loved	Goal of the Love	Dangers of the Love
affection	family, people nearby	support and nurture	holding onto security, refusal to grow up or let others grow up
friendship	people like us	shared vision and goals	exclusiveness, sharing poor values, feeling superior to different people
romance	person who feels like "other" half	completion and fulfillment of oneself	isolation from other people, idolizing the lover
love of God	highest value one can think of	gift of oneself to the highest value	holding an inadequate understanding of God, seeing oneself as more important to God than others
self-love	oneself and one's life	appreciation and fulfillment of oneself	selfishness, narcissism, self-preoccupation
agape, or love of others	humankind as a whole	unselfish service to any and all	fostering dependence, rewarding poor coping, "loving" for wrong motives

brother and sister and mother to me" (see Mark 3:31ff.,
Phillips).

FRIENDSHIP

"Birds of a feather flock together" is about friendship;
you know a lot about a person by knowing who her
friends are. Friends share similar values and goals.
Because the genders have been socialized differently,
this love is easiest between people of the same gender.
Sometimes it is erroneously associated with homosexuality. Since sex-role stereotyping is declining, friendships
between the genders should become more common than
in the past.

Many people use the term *friend* very loosely—to refer
to all people they know, or those with whom they share
activities. True friendship requires shared vision and
striving together to realize it; ideally such a bond would
unite all members of a church.

Judas' treatment of Jesus describes friendship's most
painful possibility: betrayal by someone who shared
your vision. Its biggest dangers are friends' closing out
other, different people in their enjoyment of a similar
other, or their sharing unworthy ideals with which to
inspire each other.

ROMANCE

Romantic love gets attached to someone who seems
able to "complete" you. This love is usually heterosex-
ual; however, some people's erotic impulses go out to
members of their own gender. Most psychologists believe sexual preference is not a matter of choice and gets
set early in life.

Many myths suggest that humans are split in two, and
must find their other half to be whole. You crave being
united in every possible way with another who com-
pletes you. Some people reduce this desire for union to

mere sexual interest—and equate sexual desire and love. Religions often fear romantic love and sexuality because they can absorb us so.

Some people really think they are only a part person without a mate. They manage romantic love more poorly than those who feel entire in themselves. A whole person has much more to offer a partner and doesn't need to "own" the other person.

LOVE OF GOD
Love of God is often described as yearning for the highest good. Some people fear they don't love God if they don't feel anything. However, behavior is more important than feeling. Religious traditions all define how a lover of God should and should not act, although they have some differing opinions.

Even love of God has dangers. Intolerance of those who see God differently sometimes leads to mistreating them or trying to control their behavior to make it as you think it should be. Some people get so absorbed in the idea of God as their "special lover" that they feel they are more important to God than other people. An entire church or religion may share this feeling. Belief that God has specially selected them or given them special treatment encourages such attitudes.

LOVE OF SELF

Understanding self-love is important, since we need it to be able to love at all. Many people don't know what appropriate self-love is, and hurt themselves with faulty self-love.

SELF-LOVE AND SELFISHNESS
Some people equate self-love with selfishness. They believe that to love others properly they must not consid-

er themselves at all. However well-intentioned it may be, advice not to consider yourself is poor advice. Sometimes your needs, as one human being among others, require priority. People unable to so love themselves typically don't love others appropriately either.

Selflessness. Selflessness is a tricky concept. Many religions claim that the seed must fall into the ground and die to find real life. Such selflessness requires that we keep ourselves in perspective, do not overvalue or undervalue our own desires, and are willing to pass up luxuries for higher values. We must recognize that we have been given all we have, and have no claim on it. We must surrender "forcing" things to be as we prefer, and accept the givens of our lives. Proper self-love—a recognition of our true value, and a desire to be fully what we are meant to be and live fully the lives given us—is part of true selflessness. We do not single ourselves out for *any* special treatment—either good *or* bad.

Self-love and selfishness are opposites. People who love themselves properly do not show the unhappiness, hostility, and self-preoccupation of selfish people. People who misunderstand selflessness often try to avoid selfishness maladaptively, and only enhance it in disguised and subtle ways. They may mistakenly equate selflessness with putting themselves last, impatience with themselves, or self-depreciation.

Putting Oneself Last. A truly loving person treats herself as respectfully and considerately as others—no more and no less. One who puts herself last, calling it love, often is trying to convince herself of her own goodness. "Using" loving behavior this way is an inappropriate attempt to bolster self-esteem. Such "martyrs" frequently become bitter and resentful, looking down on others who do not match their standards.

Trudy always went to the end of every line. She tended others' needs before her own, and said that JOY means putting Jesus first, then others, and then yourself. As Trudy tried to be selfless this way, her own unmet needs demanded responses from others she did not always get. Resentment welled up when people did not appreciate her unselfishness. Sometimes Trudy tried unobtrusively to draw attention to a kindness not noticed. However, her inner emptiness grew, and she increasingly resented those she was trying to love for being able to feel good about themselves while not trying so hard as she. When Trudy finally saw a therapist, she could not understand why she was angry most of the time at almost everyone. She described herself as unselfish and loving in spite of her puzzlement about her anger. Trudy had made the bad mistake of equating self-love with selfishness. By refusing to love herself, she gradually became unable to love at all. She tried to draw water out of an empty well!

Impatience with Self. Some people trying to be unselfish become demanding and impatient with themselves. They also mistakenly equate selfishness and self-love. Many suffer from love's greatest obstacle: fear. They fear being found inadequate, inferior, or "wrong." They fear that if they relax at all, they will become seriously selfish. Such people may feel "right" only when uncomfortable, suffering, or limiting themselves. They feel they do not measure up, and must "earn" their every right.

Aggie keeps strict self-discipline. She sees idle hands as the devil's workshop, and can relax only when no work is waiting. She cares for her family well, keeps her house immaculate, and exercises and eats properly. Her image is of perfection, but Aggie berates herself for laziness, untidiness, and wasting time. Her attempts at selflessness—trying to devote herself unselfishly to what she thinks she ought to be doing—have a reverse effect. She is constantly preoccupied with herself, and other people are just duties competing with other duties for her time.

Self-Depreciation. Some people consider self-deprecia- tion a necessary antidote for selfishness. However, peo- ple who depreciate themselves typically have so little self-love that they fear any attack on it. Their self- depreciation is often an attempt to protect themselves by warding off criticism. They hope that others will contra- dict their self-criticism; unfortunately, what praise they draw from others does not enhance self-esteem. The self- depreciator "knows" that she is manipulating, and can- not accept as true anything good said about her.

Iris quickly criticized everything she did, pointing out all its flaws before anyone else could comment. At first, people tried to console her by pointing to positive aspects of things she depreciated. Eventually, they tired of reassuring her and stopped it. Iris started lying to avoid situations where others might criticize her. She could not understand why, when so critical of herself, she lied to avoid others' criticism. Iris had to recognize the very strong self-concern behind her efforts to avoid self-centeredness. She wanted only to appear selfless, and was terrified of feedback that would require any real change in herself. Because she didn't have proper self- love, she couldn't accept honest help toward becoming more truly selfless.

Faulty Self-Love

Trudy, Aggie, and Iris all deceived themselves in important ways. Iris couldn't deal with her need for approval until she recognized it. Her self-protective lying finally made lying to herself impossible. Trudy's anger helped her realize that she cannot love others as she thought she did because she doesn't love herself.

Aggie will be unable to love until she acknowledges her intense self-preoccupation. Their unhelpful attempts to avoid selfishness are faulty ways of loving themselves.

Most harmful ways we try to love ourselves involve self-deceit so we can feel good about ourselves. These defense mechanisms distort our perception and make it impossible for us to deal with real issues about ourselves that need change.

Denial. Denial means blotting out unpleasant things by simply saying they aren't there—like the ostrich's burying its head in the sand. The philosopher Nietzsche explained it: when memory says I did it, and pride says I could not have done it, pride wins out in the end. "I can't believe I ate the whole thing" becomes "I didn't eat the whole thing." We are often initially aware of distorting the truth, but after we do it long enough we believe our own lies.

A small denial can become such a distortion that it is hard to see how the denier can really believe it. Norma started taking money from petty cash, telling herself she was borrowing it. She occasionally put small amounts back. When a serious shortage was discovered, she admitted her "borrowing" but insisted she had always paid it back. Although Norma probably consciously believes this, she also likely recognizes the truth "underneath" and might develop symptoms that show her interior discomfort.

Projection. Projection works like a movie projector. The picture is really in the projector, but we see it as if it were on the screen. When we project, we see our own motives and feelings as if they are in someone else. A common case occurs when you vaguely feel that someone is angry with you, but you cannot put your finger on why she should be. The chances are very good that you are angry, but read it as coming from her. Asking yourself why you may be annoyed with her will likely reveal the anger and its source.

Projection is the basis of all scapegoating. It allows us to see the causes for problems as outside ourselves. Whenever someone blames another for characteristics that describe the complainer, projection may be occurring. Julie cannot get along with her neighbor. She complains that Rosie is a busybody who wants to know about and control everything in the neighborhood. Since nobody else has problems with Rosie, Julie's own motives—which she sees as Rosie's—are likely the basis of the trouble. Julie, of course, cannot deal with Rosie until she recognizes that what she blames Rosie for are her own flaws.

Displacement. Displacing is taking out a feeling on someone other than the real target. Sometimes being honest about a feeling is frightening, so we blot out awareness of it. Then we find an excuse to let it out on a safe target. The classic example given is when a man, humiliated by his boss, cannot admit his anger for fear of losing his job. He yells at his wife about some trivial things; afraid of him, she scolds the kid. The kid, in turn, kicks the dog who chases the cat who shreds a pillow to pieces.

Patrice's job requires her to please very demanding customers who often irritate her greatly. She has convinced herself that she enjoys dealing with these people. However, the members of her dinner club notice that she has become increasingly picky about the club's schedule and is easily angered by small annoyances that never bothered her before. Patrice is displacing.

Reaction Formation. In reaction formation, we take on attitudes and behavior that are the opposite of our real inclinations to overcome tendencies in ourselves we don't like. Unfortunately, to keep our tendencies out of awareness, we often become overbearing and unfair with others who show those inclinations. People who overdo reaction formation are very rigid and hostile. Reformers out to "get" sinners often use it. Those very harsh with homosexuals, drinkers, lazy people, nonchurchgoers, etc., probably are trying to avoid knowing their own related urges.

Reaction formation looks like protesting a bit too much! We try to keep ourselves pointed in a direction that is increasingly hard to maintain—and do it in a self-dishonest way. Wanda talked about the beauty of wifely submission the most insistently just before she realized she couldn't live with that ethic anymore.

Compensation. With compensation we hide our limitations from ourselves and others by distracting from them. A student unsure of herself socially may throw all her efforts into studies; she has an excuse to avoid social involvements where her limitations would become obvious. Someone unsure of her mental abilities may become a striking dresser. Often the young women in my classes who are least sure of themselves wear excessive makeup.

Sarah is an excellent public speaker. She is very confident when on a stage with a prepared speech and an audience. At her church's functions, she tries to give directions, organize things, or have another clearly structured task. Most people would be very surprised to learn how fearfully Sarah shrinks from greeting people informally or making small talk. Sarah herself would be surprised. Developing talents that keep her from such roles lets her see herself as socially comfortable. Of course, avoiding her social fears keeps Sarah from resolving them. She maintains her self-deception by doing only tasks where she feels confident.

Rationalization. Rationalizing is justifying our behavior with motives that sound good, but are not our actual motives. This lets us explain away many failures or misdeeds. Signs of rationalization are saying things like "Everybody does it," "She needed to be taken down a few pegs," "The time wasn't right," or "I was only trying to help." We rationalize when honesty would threaten our self-esteem.

Bonnie had hoped for the promotion that Karen got. When she overheard others questioning Karen's appointment because she had been with the company so short a time, she told Karen that others were questioning her competence. Karen, filled with self-doubt, told Margo how Bonnie's report had upset her. When Margo asked Bonnie about it, she replied: "I only told her for her own good. She needed to know that the workers were not behind her." Although Bonnie's real motives were evident to Margo, she had convinced herself that she had Karen's welfare in mind.

Desacralization. Desacralization is cutting down good things that are beyond us. It helps us avoid unfavorable comparisons with ourselves. We might think or say things like "I'll bet she spends all her time working and doesn't have any friends" when someone comments on another's achievements. Or "She probably neglects her children" when another's volunteer work is described. Or "I'll bet she doesn't have a brain in her head" about a very attractive woman. Or "I expect she takes it out on her family" when someone is patient and kind. We try to feel better about ourselves by refusing to appreciate a good that we don't have. Crystal makes a negative comment whenever she hears someone praised. You probably know desacralizing people like her.

APPROPRIATE LOVE OF SELF

Your own self is the person for whom you are most responsible—where your genuine love must begin. Appropriate self-love means avoiding faulty self-love and keeping yourself healthy, whole, or holy—all these words have the same root meaning—in body, mind, and spirit.

When asked how to self-actualize, Abraham Maslow replied that it is a by-product of correct living. He said that, besides avoiding self-deception, we should also be honest with others whenever we have the least little doubt. Exceptions are rare—you might not immediately tell a very nervous person that she is dying—and are never right when the motive is to avoid pain to yourself. We should also fully attend to whatever we are doing, no matter how trivial the task. We should see good where it is, and rejoice in it. Our choices should be for growth rather than for regressive fear-based ones. Some basic practices of self-love and healthy living are offered in Chapter 5.

LOVE OF HUMANITY

Love of neighbor refers to a general love of humankind different from such particular loves as affection, friendship, and romance. Once called charity, it now is often known as agape.

LOVING OUR NEIGHBORS

What Agape Is. Agape is showing care, respect, and responsibility for others simply because they are human beings. It asks no questions about divisive barriers: race, gender, age, ethnicity, creed, education, occupation, politics, etc. It assumes that everyone is worthy in spite of incidental differences in status, personality, abilities, or other such features.

Many hotly debated issues about the religious precept of agape are beyond the scope of this book. We are concerned with people with whom you have personal contact, and not humanity as a whole. However, many problem relationships—particularly those with which we must deal unwillingly—call on our capacity for agape love. We describe the attitudes it requires before looking at some mistaken ways of trying to love your neighbor.

Attitudes Needed to Love. In *The Art of Loving,* psychologist Erich Fromm explained four abilities needed to practice any art, including loving. First, self-discipline keeps us willing and able to do what we ought regardless of our inclinations. Next, concentration means giving the necessary attention to what we are doing. Then, patience helps us persevere when results do not come quickly. Finally, we need a supreme concern for becoming adept in the art. Zen masters say we are ready for enlightenment when we want it as a drowning person wants air. When you want anything that much, you learn how to get it.

Loving requires some other special characteristics. We must overcome narcissism to see things from perspectives other than our own. This takes humility, viewing ourselves objectively, neither overinflating nor depreciating ourselves. Loving requires faith that we can count on our own and others' reliability, and belief that potentials can be developed. We also need the courage to take risks. Finally, we must *act* lovingly. Wishing to love is not the same as willing it; willing demands that we take steps to bring it about. Chapter 6 will offer some suggestions.

FAULTY LOVE OF OTHERS

Just as self-love can go awry, so also can love of others. We sometimes think we are loving when we behave destructively to ourselves and others.

Compulsive Do-gooding. Yvonne tries very hard to love. When Jane was pregnant, Yvonne frequently came over to pick up her house and do whatever laundry and dishes she could find. Jane subtly tried to discourage her, but Yvonne insisted on "serving" her. She couldn't realize that Jane was very uncomfortable with her hovering. Jane finally had to tell her so, and asked her to quit coming unless invited.

People who want to love sometimes lose sight of others' real needs. Their compulsion to give becomes more important than those they claim to serve. They tend to have strong needs to be accepted, and try to "buy" love. Since others usually want to avoid them, compulsive do-gooders' own needs keep being thwarted. They become increasingly insensitive to others as their do-gooding increases. When someone will not take "no" for an answer to her offers of help, she is really being selfish. However, remembering how strongly she needs love herself may help you deal with her.

Smothering. Some people consider trying to meet all of another's needs for love. While compulsive do-gooders dump their "love" anywhere they can, smotherers usually focus on a few people. They try to be "all things" to them and usually expect total gratitude and unwavering loyalty in return. Smotherers, uncertain of their ability to love, overdo it to convince themselves and others. Dawn was almost thirty before she began to be an adult. Her mother had so smother-loved her that she hadn't learned even simple cooking or clothes care. Breaking away from her mother's expectations of her unending devotion was very hard for Dawn.

Enabling. Enabling, another misplaced love, occurs when we continue giving kindness and acceptance to others who give us only bad behavior in return. Some religious people believe that love requires them to accept such behavior, and to keep giving unconditional love. Insensitive, ungrateful, and brutal people are thus encouraged to continue acting badly because others make no demands on them. Therapists advise their friends and families to practice a "tough love" that insists on behavior improvement as a condition for staying in the relationship. This helps abusive people realize how they treat others, and motivates them for change.

Carrie took it for granted that her wishes should be gratified. However, she was seldom around when others needed her. When Mona, distressed by her father's illness, tried to talk to Carrie about it, Carrie irritatedly complained that Mona wasn't being any fun. Mona realized that her accepting such behavior helped Carrie abuse others' love. She told Carrie that she wanted their relationship, but gave examples of behavior she would no longer accept. Carrie was humble enough to accept what Mona was telling her. Mona's "tough love" helped her improve how she dealt with others.

People-pleasing. Some people consider compliance and agreeableness the way to love. Tess became very upset whenever anyone was displeased with her. Long after she realized that pleasing people is not the same as loving them, she still had to fight her compliant tendencies. Although still sensitive to disapproval, she now judges her loving by its appropriateness and not by others' reactions.

Controlling. For Lucy, loving others means making them a project. Convinced that she knows what is best for them, she works hard at explaining it to others, encouraging them in her direction, and evaluating their progress. She is seldom without advice. When others don't want to share their concerns with her, she insists that it will make them feel better. However, every sharing then becomes a chance for her to impose her viewpoints. Those who must deal with Lucy often simply agree with her, and do things their own way. Lucy then gets upset by their inability to follow through as they "ought."

Some people mistake such manipulative control for love. They seem unable simply to listen to others with caring. Every issue becomes a problem for them to solve. Such people mask their needs for power and control as acts of love.

LOVING SELF AND OTHERS

We have looked at some bases for love and at mistakes people make in trying to love. The next chapter explores loving ourselves properly, and offers help in increasing our capacity to love others.

CHAPTER 5

Becoming Able to Love

Character is simply habit long continued.
—Plutarch, *On Moral Virtue* IV

We now turn our attention to some ways to know and nurture yourself. Our focus is on general health/holiness, and on understanding and coping with emotions that cause relationship problems.

TAKING CARE OF YOURSELF

Since our focus is mainly psychological, we mention only briefly some general practices for fostering health. Good self-help books are available for assistance in putting these ideas into practice.

BODY NURTURE

Religious people sometimes overlook the importance of good physical care. However, its role in mental and spiritual health is increasingly recognized.

Nutrition. You probably can make meals that are balanced in nutrients and provide essential vitamins. You also know that abuse of drugs, including alcohol, is harmful. You might not realize that prescription drugs can also be hazardous. Drugs for stress and anxiety are usually unnecessary; you can manage tension without these drugs, which *are* addictive and have harmful side effects. However, if you are already taking minor tranquilizers and wish to stop, ask your physician how quickly it is safe to phase them out. Too quick a withdrawal can be dangerous. The same is true of drugs for sleep.

We are just becoming educated to the harm caused by too much sugar, white flour, salt, fats, caffeine, and tobacco. Sugar is powerfully mood-altering; rapid changes in blood-sugar level put you on an emotional roller coaster that makes you eager for more sugar—and the cycle starts again. Refined sugar and flours are stripped of most nutritional value. Excessive salt and fats are hard on circulation. Caffeine is an "upper" which causes little harm used sparingly; however, many people are addicted to it, and suffer side effects of the jitters and vitamin B depletion.

Exercise. Bodies were made to be used. Without exercise, muscles—including the heart—become flabby, bones lose density, and overweight is likely. Many women's late-life bone problems, such as dowager's hump and broken hips, can be prevented by exercise earlier in life to build bone density. After menopause women are more prone to heart problems; a good aerobic exercise program offers some protection. Far more women than men are overweight. Many overweight women repeatedly lose weight and put it back on. The most recent research suggests that without exercise diets tend to fail; a built-in "appestat" encourages us to eat enough to maintain present weight unless we "reset" it by exercise.

Aerobic exercise conditions the heart and lungs. Since an unexercised body needs careful preparation, do follow all the precautions in books explaining these programs. Aerobics and calisthenics also help weight control, tone muscles for a slimming effect, and build bone density. Many such programs are available on recordings. Isometric and isotonic exercises strengthen and tone muscles; they have no other value. Body work from spiritual disciplines, like hatha yoga or t'ai chi, benefit both body and spirit; besides giving bodily flexibility, they encourage emotional calmness and concentration.

Relaxation. Learning to relax will cure half your problems! It certainly makes prescriptions for anxiety and insomnia unnecessary! Many techniques are available, some on tape. Listen to a tape before buying it; some tapes have grating voices that do not help you relax. If you cannot learn to relax after some consistent practice— ten to twenty minutes a day for about a month—then biofeedback might help. Most people can do it for themselves. When I was in high school, I had tension headaches two or three times a week. Now I have not had one for so long that I wouldn't know what it feels like—a fruit of relaxation! Relaxation also helps migraine (if started before the headache develops fully), cold extremities, high blood pressure, and other stress-related disorders.

You can try this simple practice. Lie on your back on a firm surface. You will probably want a flat pillow under your head. If your lower back is tense, put another pillow under your knees. Lie with your legs about shoulder-width apart, and your arms at about a 30-degree angle to the body with palms up. Move around until you get comfortable. Then simply start counting your breaths. The trick is to keep your attention fully on only your breath, concentrating on its going in and out. You cannot practice correctly if you are planning dinner or recalling last night's television show! Although concentration on breath is the easiest to maintain, you may substitute a relaxing image if you prefer. Some people use nature images—a lake, the sky, or an open field. For others, the image of soaking in a tub of very hot water helps. Settle on one image and do not change. Since you cannot relax if you are fretting about the time—this would be paying attention to something besides your breath—set a timer to signal the end of your time or have someone call you. You are relaxed when it feels so good that you don't want to get up. Some people also feel tingling in their fingers as relaxed blood vessels dilate and more blood flows to them.

SPIRIT NURTURE

Breathing Exercises. One good aid for emotional upset is taking long, slow, deep breaths. Emotional arousal causes fast, choppy, short breaths. Calming breathing calms emotions. Some books teach other helpful practices such as diaphragmatic breathing, cleansing breaths to combat the effects of polluted air, and alternate nostril breathing for calming and relaxing.

Meditation. Meditation deepens relaxation and mental concentration. It slows body metabolism and decreases production of tension-causing substances. It is also a helpful self-discipline.

You need a quiet place without external distractions. Sit with your spine upright, close your eyes, and place your hands on your thighs. You may use a straight chair. If you sit cross-legged, get your hipbone as high as your knees; putting one or two firm cushions under your buttocks lets you maintain an erect spine without tension. To get your spine right, imagine that a cord attached to the top of your head is being pulled up; then, holding your back in that position, drop your shoulders and hips.

Many objects are suitable for meditation. Some people meditate on the sounds inside their ear. Others visualize something like a beautiful rose, a gold coin, a pearl, or a geometric shape. Still others use short, mantralike phrases. You might choose a phrase from scriptures that appeals to you. It should not be too long; seven syllables is about right.

To meditate, passively pay attention to the object. If sensory impressions—an odor or a sound—intrude, let them go by, holding your attention on your object. Do the same with thoughts, memories, or feelings. Let them "float by" without following them. If your attention strays, gently bring it back to the object.

Inspiration. Whatever inspires you should be part of your daily routine. It may be reading, music, religious practices, or other forms of spiritual nurture. This gives you a general serenity and emotional evenness that makes getting along with yourself and other people easier.

RECOGNIZING EMOTIONS AND MOTIVES

Troublesome feelings contribute greatly to relationship problems. Your oughts, your reactions to others, and your wants all have related bad feelings when they cause problems.

Often we are not aware of feelings and thoughts before we have trouble-making reactions. To prepare for exploring them, make three lists. On the first put how others see your feelings, motives, and actions. Put how you see these on the second. On the third say what you think most people are like. Be honest.

SOME GENERAL STRATEGIES

Language Usage. Our language usage gives clues about hidden feelings and motives. Phyllis starts many sentences with indefinite subjects. She said, "It hurts," when asked about a sorrow. When asked what she wanted in her job, she replied, "Well, most people expect . . . ." Phyllis' indefinite subjects probably hide her own feelings. She means "*I* hurt" when she is sorrowing, and "*I* expect . . ." in her job. Tentative agreements also hide feelings. If you say, "I guess so" or "It seems okay," you probably have reservations you are reluctant to express. If you use language these ways, I encourage you to acknowledge your feelings.

You might say, "We should go to the drugstore," when you mean, "I want to go to the drugstore." Hiding behind shoulds puts you out of touch with your preferences. Saying "I have to" or "I must" works the same. If asked, "Says who?", you would usually have to admit that nobody is coercing you; it is a choice you made. Distinguishing between "can't" and "won't" is also important. Often "I can't" really means "I'm not willing to" or "I don't really want to"—in other words, "I won't."

Speaking apologetically indicates feeling undeserving or inferior. Frequent apologies are one clue; Lily says, "I'm sorry" when somebody else bumps into her! A friend said she apologizes for being alive. Asking permission is similar. Georgia starts many sentences with "Let me": "Let me tell you about the movie I saw last night." She hides her wish to tell behind permission-asking.

Focusing. The focusing technique was developed by Eugene Gendlin. It uses body awareness to get feelings awareness. Suppose you are "on edge" and don't know why. First you relax. Then you slowly become aware of where in your body you usually feel emotions. For example, you might usually feel sadness as a lump in your throat. At each place, pause and ask yourself how you are feeling. Wait to see what comes and give it time to take shape, then try to name it. You probably won't be quite right the first time, but play around with it. Thoughts about the feeling will also likely come and suggest some event, problem, or area of your life. Pay attention to all that comes. When another special feeling arises, focus on it. Let all ideas and images come that want to. If the feeling wants to change, let it. Continue checking other places in your body where you usually have feelings.

Following such a process will eventually lead you to a "That's it!" feeling. When you find what is disquieting you, your entire body will suddenly lighten and loosen. You have some resolution or closure on your unsettled state. This technique is especially good when you cannot sort out how you really feel. It takes practice to become good at it.

Outcomes. Often the same results occur over and again for us; things usually end the same. Noelle often gets sick just before a big party. Fay tends to get laryngitis when she must report to the board. When patterns like this occur in your life, they can tell you things about your feelings you might not know. Noelle may not really like parties, but can't admit it. Fay probably fears making reports. Deborah realized that she doesn't want to get married, because she started fighting with her fiancé as soon as they got engaged. When a feeling is too painful to admit, we often change it into other symptoms or actions that accomplish what we would want if we acknowledged the feeling.

Feedback. When others see us in ways we do not see ourselves, that can help our self-understanding. They could be correct about feelings we are hiding from ourselves. However, since we handle uncomfortable feelings in various ways, others often think we are operating from entirely different feelings and motives than we really are. We consider this problem next.

Fear and anger—with ourselves or others—make major relationship problems. These emotions rev us up—ready for "fight or flight." Neither option improves relationships! Box 5.1 lists some problem feelings in each category, how they may distort your perception of others, and how others may misread them in you. If you know your feelings, or how you often see others, this chart shows how others may misperceive you. Or, from what others say of you, you can recognize feelings you might not have realized you have.

Anger at Self. Because Lenore often feels unable to handle things and thinks others could do a better job, she begs off many tasks. Others think her uncooperative and unwilling to share her talents. She, in turn, thinks they consider themselves above her, and this strengthens her feelings of inferiority.

Sonia feels tired most of the time; everything requires a lot of effort. She has felt sad and hopeless for so long that she doesn't even realize she is depressed. Because she sees everyone else as better, more efficient, and more deserving, she shrinks from contact with others. They consider her self-centered and ignore her; she then feels even more hopeless.

Rachel is ashamed of her appearance, and does not feel able to improve it. She thinks others are as sensitive to her flaws as she is. She avoids situations that might "show her up," so others see her as unsociable and do not reach out to her. This increases her feelings of not matching up.

Ida cannot forget the things she has done against her values. She blames herself, and thinks others would

BOX 5.1
REACTIONS TO BAD FEELINGS

If You Feel:	You Are Likely to See Others as:	Others Are Likely to See You as:
	Feelings of Anger at Self	
inferior, inadequate	snobbish, haughty, acting superior	conceited, unresponsive, uncooperative
depressed, sad	better than you, superior	self-centered, smug, wanting to be alone
embarrassed, ashamed	critical, lording it over you	secretive, unsociable
guilty, self-blaming	judgmental, blaming	sneaky, angry, withdrawing
	Feelings of Anger at Others	
jealous	grabby and unloving	angry, wanting to punish
resentful	insulting, aggressive	unkind, unsympathetic
frustrated	stubborn, resistant	bossy, coercive
bored	uninteresting, tedious	rude, uncaring
irritated	uncooperative	demanding, nitpicking
	Feelings of Fear of Others	
afraid	punishing, unloving	angry, unable to make up mind
anxious	hard to please	incompetent, pushy
insecure, confused	frightening, unresponsive	anxious, stupid
alienated, isolated	closing you out	deceitful, angry, "closed"
	Feelings of Fear of Self	
shy, awkward	unfriendly, in-groupy	uninterested, aloof, wary
dependent, lonely	unkind, insensitive	demanding, hard to please
worried, indecisive	aloof, unapproachable	snobbish, self-preoccupied

judge her harshly if they knew her as she knows herself. She often acts furtively, as if about to be discovered; sometimes she flares up in anger when she feels blamed for anything. The rejection of others, who are not comfortable with her, makes her feel even less acceptable.

How most of us react when we see ourselves as an obstacle, a failure, or unworthy leads others to misread us. They often see us as smug or self-satisfied—the very opposite of how we feel! We see them as angry at us, and misunderstandings multiply.

Anger at Others. Kristi needs to "own" her friends. When she is not included when a friend is with someone else, jealousy flares. She feels cheated out of her rights. Her sulking and pouting advertise her anger indirectly. Her jealousy includes fear that the friend will find someone else more appealing and will abandon her.

Whenever Alice is not the center of attention, she considers her worth challenged. Her resentment at feeling "cut down" leads to biting remarks about those she holds responsible. Alice does not realize that others see her as unkind because she honestly feels she has a legitimate complaint.

When things do not move fast enough for her, or how she wants them to, Lorna becomes very tense. She thinks others are deliberately being stubborn or slow. She cannot relax, and tries to make things go as she wishes. Her frustration comes out as bossy coercion, and often compounds problems.

Carla thinks that life has let her down. Nothing engages or interests her. Instead of finding values that challenge herself, she has settled into considering others tedious and boring. She doesn't hide her disenchantment, and is seen as rude and uncaring.

Very little things set Kerry off. She gets annoyed and exasperated by any inconvenience or setback. Others find her very demanding, while she sees them as unco-operative and believes that her feelings are not respect-ed.

Anger toward others is sometimes justified, and needs to be dealt with openly and objectively. However, many times we hide angry feelings from ourselves or, if we recognize them, don't want others to know. We act passive-aggressively; the hostility "leaks" out. Feelings of entitlement are often the major problem. When we think something is owed us, or that things ought always be as we wish, we easily get angry; we have low frustration tolerance.

Fear of Others. Since Gloria is afraid that people will find what she says stupid, she keeps her opinions to herself. Sometimes she surprises everyone with an angry flare-up; neither she nor others realize that her fearful desire for acceptance was so burdensome that she changed it into the easier emotion of anger at being unheard.

Ursula usually feels generally uncomfortable in social situations; we call this emotion anxiety because she cannot pinpoint what bothers her. Her apprehensive expectation of something bad makes others seem hard to please. She looks pushy when she tries to force herself past her anxiety, and incompetent when it makes her unable to act.

General insecurity and confusion describe Wendy's feelings. She also looks stupid at times because, feeling unsafe and not knowing what is expected, she bogs down. She would like guidance from others, but sees them as unresponsive.

Ellen is alienated. She feels closed out by others, not a real part of any group's activities. Her attempts to protect herself in this painful isolation make others see her as "closed" to them. As they ignore her, her sense of utter aloneness increases.

Fear of others often has the very sad effect of making others afraid of us! They may fear rejection by us, or that our apparent uncertainty will mess up situations. Sometimes they fear that we will become burdensome to them. As both sides back off, problems do not get resolved.

Fear of Self. Shy people negatively evaluate themselves and expect others to share this evaluation. Violet avoids others' negative reactions by withdrawing. Although she longs to socialize, she considers others an in-group with no room for her. They see her as aloof and uninterested in them.

Opal greatly needs to have people around. She cannot tolerate being alone for any length of time. Her need leads her to make many demands on others, and to seem never satisfied with what she gets. As others draw back from her excessive neediness, they look insensitive and unkind to her. She desperately tries even harder, driving them away even more strongly.

Trixie frets and worries about how to handle situations. Because she is so wrapped up in her thoughts, others think her snobbishly self-preoccupied and unwilling to negotiate. They avoid her, leaving her with few clues about how to interact with them. Their unapproachability leaves her even more unsure of what to do.

People with many doubts about themselves often act in ways that lead others to confirm these doubts. They strongly need affirmation, and do things that bring strong disconfirmation.

DEALING WITH PROBLEM FEELINGS

Although we usually plan our actions from feelings, thoughts of which we are often unaware lie behind them. Our previous behavior helped shape these thoughts. The chain of behavior-thoughts-feelings-motives-behavior can keep us digging more deeply into negative patterns. Fortunately, we can interrupt the chain and make it work positively for us.

MANAGING THE THOUGHTS BEHIND OUR FEELINGS

Psychologists call our first method cognitive restructuring. It helps us deal with just about any problem feeling.

Uncovering Negative Ideas. First we must find our negative thinking. Most of us are unaware of what we tell ourselves to foster bad feelings. However, every bad feeling is supported by thinking. Albert Ellis calls it the ABC pattern: A = activating event, B = irrational belief, and C = consequential emotion.

Start work by catching yourself in a bad feeling. Working on it immediately, while you still have the feeling, is best. If you cannot, do so as soon as possible. You need a pen and a notepad. In your imagination put yourself back into the situation that spurred the feeling. Start writing whatever comes into your mind. If you can't think of what to say, start by writing that down. Just keep writing, no matter what you say. Eventually you will start writing thoughts related to the feeling. Some of them may look quite bizarre to you. Don't censor anything; write them just as they come. Nobody will see this but you. With practice, you can get so you hardly know what you are writing until you reread it. This is the very best work because you have successfully turned off your mental censors that make you evaluate what you say.

When Thea didn't call her as agreed, Nita wrote: "Well, she's not going to call now—it's too late. There I go again. Why can't I ever keep a friend? As soon as I count on someone, she drops me. It's not too much to ask someone to call when she says she will. I might as well forget the whole mess. Nobody's ever really cared about me anyway. I'll probably never have a friend I can really count on. What's wrong with me? I sure do my damndest. Nobody appreciates how hard I try. Can't someone take a little pity on me? If I was dying of thirst, they probably wouldn't even give me a drop of water. Sometimes I wonder why I even hang around. They'd probably all feel guilty if they saw me in my coffin—or would they even care at all? They probably wouldn't even bother to come, and my parents would be so embarrassed because the whole world would know their daughter is a social flop."

Nita wrote more, but this gives a sample. These thoughts support the mixture of feelings churning around inside her. Note how one small event—the failure of a friend to call—led to her seeing herself as a total failure, condemned to aloneness and misunderstanding the rest of her life.

Ellis says that after the ABC, we move to D (disputing responses) and E (positive effects). To start, Nita listed times she failed to phone when she said she would, and why she didn't. She saw for herself that many different reasons might be behind Thea's not calling. The next time a friend didn't call, she could remember these reasons. However, even if Thea were avoiding her, Nita had to see how absurd the conclusions she drew were. I asked her what it would be like if Thea proved not to be a friend. She said that it would be terrible; she couldn't take it. We changed that to: "I would really dislike it. I prefer for Thea to be my friend." Getting perceived consequences in perspective is important. One person's rejection doesn't mean a lifetime of loneliness!

We then picked out the main irrational beliefs that kept Nita feeling resentment, alienation, and shame. We put disputing responses for them on index cards; one copy of each went on Nita's bedroom mirror, and another into her purse. Every time she saw the cards, she repeated the ideas to herself. Some disputing responses Nita used were: "I can't judge the future by the past," "I can act like a friend," "I don't have to please my parents," "I have gifts to offer," and "Not everybody has to like me."

Rehearsing reasonable ideas to replace irrational ones stops our self-talk from leading to bad emotions and inappropriate action. Doing cognitive restructuring prepares you to cope more adequately. A therapist can help if you get stuck or cannot develop disputing responses.

WORKING WITH PARTICULAR FEELINGS

Cognitive restructuring helps with all negative feelings. Some additional ideas work well for particular bad feelings.

Anger at Self. Unrecognized anger can immobilize you or lead to irate outbursts. The tired and bogged-down feelings of anger at yourself (depression, guilt) can be helped by vigorous activity—even as short as a brisk walk around the block. If you are prone to such feelings, an exercise program is especially helpful. Sugar is very bad for you, and should be avoided as much as possible.

Sometimes bad past behavior causes anger at yourself. O. Hobart Mowrer said that we *are* our secrets; that is, our self-esteem depends on what we keep secret. He urged depressed or guilty people to confess their faults to involved others. If harm has been done, work out recompense. Unfortunately, most of us keep such things secret when we can, and destroy self-esteem. Mowrer also encouraged keeping secret some good things we do. This builds a reservoir of good secrets, and we feel good about ourselves. These ideas came from Lloyd Douglas' *Magnificent Obsession,* based on the first verses of Matthew 6. They are also important in the Anonymous programs— Alcoholics Anonymous, Overeaters Anonymous, etc. They allow us to let go of the past, and live in the present feeling good about ourselves.

Another good idea is to develop a list of your assets. Put down anything good you can about yourself, being sure to include what others have complimented you on. Add things as you think of them. Read your list when you are down on yourself. Make another list of all your shoulds—what you tell yourself you must do. Then, for each one, ask what the consequences will be one week, one month, or one year from now if you don't do it. Permit yourself to eliminate unnecessary shoulds.

Fear of Self. Fears about yourself can be defused by the list of assets discussed above. Relaxation and meditation also help. Paying attention to others can reduce self-consciousness. Try to put at ease others who look nervous, shy, or alone. Remember to smile at others and avoid having your arms folded across your chest or your eyes to the ground—these block out others.

One very important technique is thought-stopping. This can help for any bad feeling, but works especially well here. Set a timer for about two minutes, then sit and think your negative thoughts. When the timer goes off, yell "Stop" at yourself, and halt the thinking. Reset the timer and repeat the procedure. Do this half a dozen times a day until you can turn the thoughts off whenever you wish just by saying "Stop." When negative thoughts occur at other times, say "Stop" to yourself—silently, of course, if in public. With a little practice, you can stop negative thinking with a word!

Anger at Others. If you are angry at others, work on your sense of entitlement. Recognize how you expect more for yourself than other people. Self-talk cards help change such attitudes. Vigorous exercise and avoiding stimulants also help. You can build frustration tolerance by deliberately delaying small indulgences like a snack or larger ones like buying a new car. Record the situations that trigger your anger, and plan alternate ways to handle them. When frustrated, you might scrub floors hard; when irritated, you might jog. You can also excuse yourself from situations where you want to dominate or demand from others.

Fear of Others. Two techniques useful for most fears are flooding and desensitization. Blanche desensitized her fear of disagreeing with others. She listed feared possibilities beginning with the least frightening: disagreeing with something written in a book. She filled in various other scenes—each a little more fear-producing than the last—up to the most feared: publicly disagreeing with someone. She thoroughly relaxed by counting her breaths, then imagined the book scene. As soon as anxiety started, she went back to watching her breath. When she could think of the book situation without tension, she went on to the next and worked her way up the list—always going back to breath awareness when she felt anxious. After several weeks of daily practice, she had reached the top of her list and could comfortably disagree with another person in public.

In flooding, you face and stay in the feared experience until all anxiety disappears. Edna was afraid to go to church alone. She forced herself to go as far as she could—to the corner of the block—and stood there until her fear disappeared. Then she walked to within a block of the church. She was still standing there with some fear when the service ended. As people walked toward her the fear rose again, but she stood firm and greeted those she knew. The next week, she got as far as the church door—after the service had started. In two more weeks, she happily walked to church alone and on time. With this technique you must stay in the situation until all fear disappears. Leaving makes the problem worse because the relief of escape makes escaping more likely the next time.

PREPARING FOR RELATIONSHIP ISSUES

The next task is applying newfound self-awareness and emotional comfort to managing problems. There are tactics for advance preparation, and others for emergency use in problem situations.

ADVANCE PREPARATIONS

You are doing self-talk with disputing responses, and may have tried other suggestions for your particular bad feelings. These, and the practices opening this chapter, are your remote preparation. For immediate preparation, list the situations that usually bring bad feelings, how you typically handle them, and what your results are.

For each situation, define the outcomes you want and decide what behavior is most likely to get these results. Picture yourself acting that way, and note what feelings arise. If they are familiar ones, you already have some disputing responses for the negative thoughts sustaining them. If a new bad feeling comes, go through the cognitive restructuring steps.

Use the self-talk cards that fight these feelings frequently for several days before the situation. Also rehearse what you need to say and do, anticipating likely responses. Try to get a friend to role-play probable scenes with you. Rehearse until you feel comfortable. Promise yourself a reward if you follow through—and keep your promise!

IN A BAD SITUATION

If a situation still swamps you with bad feelings, do not be dismayed. Don't expect immediate change in yourself. Do remember to breathe slowly and deeply, and to admit your feelings to yourself. Say to yourself your disputing responses for these feelings. If you cannot drown out negative ideas, use thought-stopping. (To make it work, you must have practiced it before.) Recall your goals, and what you need to do to reach them. Continue to monitor your breathing, and use positive self-talk. When able, begin tackling the situation again.

CONFLICT RESOLUTION

If your goals put you at variance with others, good conflict resolution can prevent bitterness. Invite the other person to sit down with you, preferably privately, to identify the causes of your conflict. Sometimes you will find you have different goals, or prefer different methods to reach the same goal. Your expectations of yourselves and others may be different. These problems can usually be resolved by negotiation and compromise if everyone is willing to be both honest and fair. A resolution that does not define a clear winner and loser is important. Each person should get some things that she wants; a "win-win" strategy makes possible further harmonious dealing with each other.

The situation is trickier when the conflict is caused by somebody's bad feelings. If they are yours, you already know what to do. If they are the other person's, be sensitive to her pain and try to minimize it. The next chapter talks about people whose characteristics or situations make bad feelings—yours or theirs—likely to occur in your dealings with each other.

CHAPTER 6

Managing Special People

Nothing human is foreign to me.
—Terence, *Heautontimorumenos*
(The Self-Tormentor) I. i.

We now turn to touchy relationships. Sometimes people's characteristics or behavior makes accepting them difficult for you. Sometimes their circumstances make feeling accepted and fairly treated hard for them. This chapter should help you deal with them more effectively, kindly, and cooperatively.

SOME GENERAL PRINCIPLES

How we think and act sets the stage for later feelings about others. We look first at ideas helpful in all problem cases.

DIFFERENT BACKGROUNDS

We each bring a unique background to our current life. Our different genetic endowments affect intelligence, temperament, stamina, and abilities. We also all have different early life experiences and guiding fictions (Chapter 2). The more these guide our understanding and conduct, the harder it becomes to recognize what contradicts them as validly human.

For each person we have trouble accepting, the odds are very good that we would be as she is were all the things that went to form us exactly like hers. The saying "There but for the grace of God go I" captures this understanding. We have incomplete freedom to choose how we manage our lives. General human limitations of body and spirit plague us, apart from those which are consequences of our own past actions.

Because Vicki has smoked heavily, saying "No" to a cigarette is harder for her than for Betty, who decided not to continue after a few months of smoking. But, before the consequences of her past smoking, Vicki had greater biological or emotional susceptibility to smoking. She may have had some control at some time over these circumstances, or she may not. Human choice is simply too complex to expect another to change problem behavior at will. An American Indian saying tells us to walk a mile in another's moccasins before judging.

BEHAVIOR AND ATTITUDES

Attitudes tend to follow behavior, according to cognitive dissonance theory (Chapter 2). Changing attitudes is easier after we do things that reflect the attitudes we want to hold. This principle was behind forced racial integration in the United States. Making people interact with other races changed attitudes faster than trying to sell them on equality. Actual loving behavior will change your attitudes faster than trying to convince yourself to be more tolerant.

Try also to separate the person from the characteristics you don't like. Little acts of kindness show acceptance of the person whose features disturb you. Alicia, a pastor, counsels abortion clients. She is unhappy about the women who picket the clinic, believing they inflict emotional hurt on other women who are already suffering. However, on a hot day, she took a cold drink out to a picketer whom she overheard complaining of thirst. When Alicia left the clinic an hour later, the woman nodded at her, possibly now able to believe that she was not all bad.

SOME PARTICULAR PROBLEMS

We will discuss problem relationships under large general headings. Although you have no trouble dealing with some people discussed, others do. If you have a problem not dealt with, decide under which general heading it falls and study what is said there.

RELIGIOUSLY DIFFERENT PEOPLE

Ideas for Thought. Our environment powerfully shapes our religious beliefs. We are taught religious ideas as young children, and most of us change our perspectives very little. Early understandings of ourselves, the world, and others have so shaped us that they greatly limit the religious ideas possible for us to adopt. If an ardent Shi'ite Muslim tried to convince you that her faith was absolutely essential for your spiritual well-being, you probably could not convert even if you wished to. If you tried to convince her similarly of your beliefs, you would likely fail. People are usually ripe for such conversions only when their lives are in upheaval. Similarly, were you born in the heart of India, you probably would not hold the religious beliefs you do. If you now have a devotional love of Jesus, you would probably be similarly devoted to Krishna. Transcending cultural limits is very difficult.

Milton Rokeach suggested looking at religion in terms of those who care, regardless of their particular beliefs and practices, and those who do not. Although this helps us deal with different faiths, or different styles (fundamental or liberal) of our own faith, it does not help us deal with the irreligious. They, however, were also subject to early formative experiences that left them as they now are.

Ideas for Action. If someone tries to persuade you to her opinions, simply say that you are satisfied with your own beliefs. Trying to impose religious opinions on another is insensitive to her right to determine her own worldview. Religious argument persuades only those who want to be persuaded. Friendly debate is possible, but difficult unless both parties respect the other's position and are sensitive to feelings. If differing religious perspectives make trouble in dealing with someone, try inviting her to explain her faith to you. It is probably important enough to her that you will be able to appreciate how it informs her life if you let her share it. If you want to object to anything she says, remember that you could now be in her position but for accidental circumstances of life. You might also help her practice her faith by offering transportation, child care, or other services that make it easier. Such caring will foster your acceptance of her.

"IMMORAL" PEOPLE

General Considerations. We differ in what we consider immoral, and this also depends greatly on what we were taught when young. Marcia cannot understand Pauline's values. She was taught that sexual behavior without contraceptives is irresponsible unless you are trying to conceive a child. Pauline grew up believing that contraception is sinful, and that one should always willingly accept the consequences of sexual activity. Marcia can accept Pauline although she doesn't agree with her. Since she wants to treat Pauline well, she does not try to convince her that her own beliefs are better.

Most of us are not morally consistent. Elise strongly opposes abortion, believing that it destroys innocent life.

Yet wars in which innocent civilians, including children, are killed do not bother her. Rosalie argues that one ought not be forced to have her body used as a life-support system for another against her will. Yet she considers Jessica's twin immoral for refusing to donate a kidney Jessica needs. Other people's inconsistencies make us think they are operating in bad faith. We usually are not aware of our own, and would try to explain them away were they pointed out to us.

We also use arguments selectively to support our positions—sometimes out of context. Few Christians would cut off a hand with which they were tempted to sin, yet many hold that remarriage after divorce is adultery, citing Scripture passages not far from those recommending self-mutilation to avoid sin. We can argue endlessly about what to take literally in Scripture and what not. Note, however, that such choices commonly are made to support positions already adopted.

Dealing with Those You Consider Immoral. Two areas with many bad feelings are abortion and homosexuality. Many consider those people who differ from them a danger to society. Yet many varied life experiences underlie your and others' decisions about abortion. Homosexuality seems even more basic; we don't know what causes sexual preference, but it is established quite young in life and is seldom, if ever, a matter of choice. Many sincerely religious gays and lesbians cannot believe that God, who made them as they are, expects them to live their lives without sex.

How can you deal comfortably with people who differ morally? Try to understand why they feel as they do, assuming their good faith as you want them to assume yours. You need not condone moral choices repugnant to you, or foster their practice. However, adopting condemning or punitive attitudes attacks the person and not her behavior. When you try to impose your morality on others, you take from them rights that you want to retain for yourself. Protecting victims or repairing abuses caused by others' behavior does not require punishing them. For example, depriving homosexuals of civil rights attacks the person, not the behavior.

Dealing with Those Who Condemn You. If others consider you immoral, sensitivity to their deeply ingrained morality can make you more acceptable to them. Unfortunately, some people choosing nontraditional values do so in a defiant manner that outrages others. Since going against prevailing societal standards is always difficult, you probably suffered some indecision or agonizing over your choice. Acknowledging this lets your opponents know that you are not heedlessly discarding standards important to them. Self-honesty may even require your admitting some uncertainty now; this does not nullify your conclusions, but protects you from the dogmatism or legalism you may dislike in your opponents.

A wise person once advised me on moral choices contrary to accepted values. You might wish to apply the advice to some of your dilemmas. First, consult the scriptures of your tradition. Don't worry that you can always read them to support your position; we all do that. Second, consult a knowledgeable spokesperson for the tradition; again, you can always find someone to agree with you. However, these sources may also offer additional ideas to ponder. Third, ask with your deepest self-honesty if you truly think the action acceptable. If so, then ask if you are willing to pay, *without resentment,* the costs of this deviance. If that answer is also yes, then feel free to follow your choice. Although society is maintained by people's shared values, all moral advances come from those with a different vision and the courage to follow it. If you bear the costs of such a

decision without resentment, your compassionate understanding of those holding more conservative values
should go a long way toward easing relationships with
them.

ACTIVISTS/PROTESTERS

Environmentalists, feminists, socialists, antiwar protesters, and others seeking societal change often draw
the anger of those who accept the status quo. They are
similarly angered by these others.

Understanding Protesters. Most protesters consider society to have ills they want cured. They may be suffering
from them or acting out of compassion for sufferers. If
you are privileged in what others want changed, you may
easily resent their arguments for a different way. Those
who benefit from the status quo prefer not to have the
boat rocked. You can ease your dealings with activists by
understanding how your advantages in a situation make
finding anything wrong with it difficult.

Activists may threaten your security. Even if things
don't entirely satisfy you, you may fear that change could
bring worse conditions or require accommodation to
unknown possibilities. Many fearful people feed their
fears with erroneous beliefs instead of seeking accurate
information. Be open to the facts.

Hilda would have nothing to do with feminists. She
insisted that their demands would destroy the moral
fiber of the country since they wanted to change the God-
given order between the sexes. She saw the Equal Rights
Amendment as bringing unisex toilets, making women
hold unwanted jobs, causing women to be drafted, and
forcing women to have undesired abortions. She
wouldn't let people explain to her the errors in these
opinions. She also said that women should let men worry
about equal pay and opportunity. When Hilda was left by

her husband at age forty, without job skills, feminism looked better to her. She recognized that fear of change— of having responsibilities she felt she could not handle— and resentment that younger women have options she did not had supported her former beliefs. Her objections had been rationalizations (Chapter 4) protecting her from painful feelings.

Handling Those Who Support the Status Quo. A helpful start in dealing with those who resist change is appreciation of how they may be threatened. A gentle rather than demanding attitude also helps. Some activists fail to appreciate others' rights, thus causing unnecessary conflict. Jane Loevinger (Chapter 3) says that distinguishing preconformists from postconformists is difficult, since both act against conformity. However, preconformists have not learned to appreciate others' rights, while sensitivity to others is evident in postconformist reformers. Making sure a proposed action fairly treats others clothes your activism in agape love.

OFFENSIVE LIFE-STYLES

Social conventions are so important to some people that they attach moral connotations to them. Not long ago, boys were barred from schools until they got a short haircut and girls were similarly treated for wearing slacks. Some people considered such deviance a sign of moral deterioration. Virtually any life-style can bother someone, but those people usually seen as most offensive are societal dropouts, those not gainfully employed, users of mood-altering chemicals, those whose sexual patterns differ from the norm, and those threatening to others.

If Others Offend You. For those who chose their life-style, the major consideration is freedom. Although you have a right to protection if they harm you, imposing your choices on them infringes on their freedom. A helpful thought is whether you would like them to dictate your life-style!

Others have not chosen to live as they do, but are victims of their own or societal dis-ease. Often personal and cultural problems interact. Many economic analysts say our society will never again be able to employ all its members. Those most limited in resources will suffer most. Although some abuse such systems as welfare, we who seek to love must ask ourselves seriously whether we could exclude our least fortunate sisters from some of society's goods. Similarly, those trapped in employment that erodes their personhood, those for whom mood-altering chemicals so dulled emotional pain that they became addicted to them, and those young people adrift in valuelessness and purposelessness need compassion as suffering parts of the larger organism that we all make up. We ought not tolerate bad behavior from them—that validates such behavior (Chapter 4)—but can approach them as wounded parts of ourselves.

If You Offend Others. When you deviate from conventional norms, you are wise to be sensitive to others' feelings. You cannot force them to approve, so you best not blatantly advertise your private business to unaccepting people. If you demand approval from others who have no business in your affairs, you probably want to antagonize them and might well examine your anger.

If you are forced—by societal or your own limitations—into a life-style you would not choose, you bear the brunt of our culture's pain. Others' insensitivity adds to your burden. It is important that you not lose determination to do for yourself what you can to improve your situation. Remaining helpless, when you could do something, causes loss of others' support you might otherwise have. Many fine centers offer treatment for addiction to alcohol, prescription medications, and street drugs. Displaced Homemakers programs offer women who must become economically self-sufficient personal counseling, career guidance, and referrals for training. Shelters for battered women offer counseling that helps stop domestic violence and abuse. An increasing number of counties and states assist in collecting child support payments.

IRRITATING HABITS

Many different personal characteristics can annoy others. They fall into two general classes: those true of many members of a particular group and those idiosyncratic to persons.

Annoying Groups. Older people typically annoyed Roxanne. She anticipated finding them burdensome. With such a set, her consistent difficulty in dealing with them is not surprising. Kim suggested to her that she may be stereotyping the elderly. Roxanne hadn't thought of this before, but was open enough to examine her attitudes. She realized that old people frightened her by reminding her that she was aging and would one day die. She volunteered at a nursing home; by meeting many different older people, she came to see them as individuals and to deal with them comfortably.

If you find most members of any group annoying, you are probably prejudiced (prejudging) against that group. Your prejudice may be learned (Chapter 2), or may rest on your fears and hopes. The cognitive restructuring exercises (Chapter 5) on the feelings the group elicits may help you see your prejudices. If this fails, therapy may help you heal this spiritual disease.

Idiosyncratic Habits. Many of our personal habits of style, speech, and action are so automatic that we are not aware of them. We must regularly deal with others whose habits differ. We are bound to find some of these annoying, especially when they impinge on us in ways we do not like. When another's habit adversely affects our well-being, we must call it to her attention. Nell frequently says: "I'd be grateful if you'd put out that cigarette. I'm getting ill from the smoke." (Notice her I-talk; Chapter 1.) Often, however, tolerating others' habits is an opportunity to exercise agape love. It helps to recall that your habits undoubtedly also annoy others at times.

People found listening to Zelda's overexplanations of almost everything very tedious. Lisa realized that Zelda might not be aware of how she comes across. She gently told her that people would understand her better with less explanation, and gave her several examples. Zelda asked Lisa to help her catch herself when she did it; within several months, Zelda improved considerably.

Honesty with a person you care about is a favor. Of course, be sure to use good communication skills (Chapter 1) in giving feedback about irksome habits. When you are dealing with someone who is not a friend, very carefully check your motives before speaking. You may be wishing more to hurt than help the gumchewer, loud talker, or messy person who is bothering you.

SOME SUMMARY IDEAS

Remember how life experiences explain many differences between you and the person next to you. You have different values, expectations, sensitivities, weak spots, and worldviews—even if similar in some ways. Your habits, style, and level of personal maturity are not exactly the same, and are based on at least some things outside your control. As you want to be accepted, so does she.

Different people call for different kinds of love and understanding from you. However, with all people the goal is cooperative, caring, and effective relationships. You can easily deceive yourself about loving because we protect ourselves from learning what upsets our opinions of ourselves. We often give a faulty pseudo love instead of acting from a reasoned examination of others' real needs. Your good detective work in figuring out the needs behind another's timidity, anger, withdrawal, pouting, anxiety, restlessness, etc., is a good start on improving your relationship with her. You can give her the drop of honey that she needs.

In talking with both old and new acquaintances, checking out what you think the other person is saying, or is feeling or thinking, prevents unfortunate misperceptions. When appropriate, you help others by leveling about your feelings, plans, motives, and thoughts, and by confronting them on behavior disruptive to your dealings with each other. To keep communication channels open, remember to use I-statements, and to sugarcoat uncomfortable messages.

Reading this book is a first step in relationship improvement. Practicing its suggestions comes next. What has been said here will help only if you actually start applying the ideas you have learned. With good effort and persistence, you can find yourself dealing much more effectively with other people.